MW01004799

THOUGHT AS A SYSTEM

In *Thought as a System*, best-selling author David Bohm takes as his subject the role of thought and knowledge at every level of human affairs, from our private reflections on personal identity to our collective efforts to fashion a tolerable civilization.

Elaborating upon principles of the relationship between mind and matter first put forward in *Wholeness and the Implicate Order*, Professor Bohm rejects the notion that our thinking processes neutrally report on what is 'out there' in an objective world. He explores the manner in which thought actively participates in forming our perceptions, our sense of meaning and our daily actions. He suggests that collective thought and knowledge have become so automated that we are in large part controlled by them, with a subsequent loss of authenticity, freedom and order.

In conversations with fifty seminar participants in Ojai, California, David Bohm offers a radical perspective on an underlying source of human conflict, and inquires into the possibility of individual and collective transformation.

The late **David Bohm** was Emeritus Professor at Birkbeck College, University of London. He was the author of many articles and books including *Causality and Chance in Modern Physics*, *Wholeness and the Implicate Order* and *The Undivided Universe* (with Basil Hiley).

THOUGHT AS A SYSTEM

David Bohm

This is a transcription of a seminar held in Ojai, California from 31 November to 2 December 1990. It has been edited by Professor Bohm.

Routledge
Taylor & Francis Group

LONDON AND NEW YORK

First published 1992
by David Bohm Seminars

This edition first published 1994
by Routledge
2 Park Square, Milton Park, Abingdon, Oxon OX14 4RN

Simultaneously published in the USA and Canada
by Routledge
711 Third Avenue, New York, NY 10017

Routledge is an imprint of the Taylor & Francis Group, an informa business

© 1994 Sarah Bohm

Phototypeset in Palatino by Intype, London

British Library Cataloguing in Publication Data
A catalogue record for this book is available from the British
Library

Library of Congress Cataloguing in Publiçation Data

Bohm, David.
Thought as a system / David Bohm
p.   cm.
Includes index.
1. Philosophy of mind. 2. Knowledge, Theory of. I. Title
BD418.3.R64   1994
128'.2–dc20   93–46728

ISBN10: 0-415-11980-4 (hbk)
ISBN10: 0-415-11030-0 (pbk)

ISBN13: 978-0-415-11980-1 (hbk)
ISBN13: 978-0-415-11030-3 (pbk)

David Bohm died in 1992.
This book is dedicated to his memory.

CONTENTS

FOREWORD

In *Thought as a System* theoretical physicist David Bohm takes as his subject the role of thought and knowledge at every level of human affairs, from our private reflections on personal identity to our collective efforts to fashion a tolerable civilization. Elaborating upon principles of the relationship between mind and matter first put forward in *Wholeness and the Implicate Order*, Dr Bohm rejects the notion that our thinking processes neutrally report on what is 'out there' in an objective world. He explores the manner in which thought actively participates in forming our perceptions, our sense of meaning and our daily actions. He suggests that collective thought and knowledge have become so automated that we are in large part controlled by them, with a subsequent loss of authenticity, freedom and order. In three days of conversation with fifty seminar participants in Ojai, California, Dr Bohm offers a radical perspective on an underlying source of human conflict, and inquires into the possibility of individual and collective transformation.

In Bohm's view, we have inherited a belief that mind (or thought) is of an inherently different and higher order than matter. This belief has nurtured a faith in what we call *objectivity* – the capacity to observe and report neutrally on some object or event, without having any effect on what we are looking at, or without being affected by it. Historically, this perspective has given us a scientific and cultural world view in which isolated, fragmentary parts mechanically interact with one another. Bohm points out that this fragmentary view corresponds to 'reality' in significant respects, but suggests that we have overextended our faith in the objectivist perspective. Once we make the critical (and false) assumption that thought and knowledge are not participating in our sense of reality, but only reporting on it, we are committed to a view that does not take into account the complex, unbroken processes that underlie the world as we experience it.

To help bring into focus thought's participatory nature, Bohm undertakes an extensive redefinition of thought itself. To begin with, thought is not fresh, direct perception. It is literally *that which has been 'thought'* – the past, carried forward into the present. It is the instantaneous display of memory, a superimposition of images onto the active, living present. On the one hand, this memory is what allows us to perform even the simplest of tasks, such as getting dressed in the morning. On the other hand, memory is also responsible for various aspects of fear, anxiety or apprehension, and the actions that proceed from these memories. Thought, then, is also inclusive of *feelings*, in the form of latent emotional experiences. Not only negative, painful emotions are folded into thought, but pleasurable ones as well. Indeed, the whole spectrum of emotions as we typically experience them is seen by Bohm as thought-related.

The manner in which feeling and thought interpenetrate one another is central to Bohm's view of the functioning of consciousness. Throughout the mind and body, he says, they form a structure of neurophysiological *reflexes*. Through repetition, emotional intensity and defensiveness, these reflexes become 'hard-wired' in consciousness, to such an extent that they respond independently of our conscious choice. If, for example, someone tells you that a member of your family is both ugly and stupid, you will most likely have instantaneous surges of adrenalin and blood pressure that are inseparable from your thought: 'He is wrong! He is rude and malicious for saying such things!' The thought 'He is wrong!' will tend to justify and perpetuate the bodily surges. Likewise, the surges will tend to certify the thought. In time, the experience will fade, but it is effectively stored in the memory and becomes 'thought'. There it waits to be instantly recalled the next time a similar situation is encountered.

In addition to emotions and reflexes, Bohm includes human artifacts in his definition of thought. Computer systems, musical instruments, cars, buildings – these are all illustrations of thought in its *fixed, concrete* form. From Bohm's perspective, to make a fundamental separation between thought and its products would be the equivalent of suggesting that whether a person is male or female is a separate phenomenon from the genetic process that determined the sex to begin with. Such a separation would in fact illustrate the very fragmentation under examination.

Finally, Bohm posits that thought and knowledge are primarily collective phenomena. Our common experience is that we have personal thoughts that come from our individual 'self'. Bohm suggests that this is a culturally inherited sensibility that overemphasizes the role of isolated parts. He inverts this view, noting that the 'flow of meaning' between people is more fundamental than any individual's particular thoughts. The individual is thus seen as an *idiosyncrasy* (literally, 'private mixture') of the collective movement of values, meanings and intentions.

The essential relevance of Bohm's redefinition of thought is the proposal that body, emotion, intellect, reflex and artifact are now understood as *one unbroken field of mutually informing thought*. All of these components interpenetrate one another to such an extent, says Bohm, that we are compelled to see 'thought as a system' – concrete as well as abstract, active as well as passive, collective as well as individual.

Our traditional world view, in an attempt to maintain a simple, orderly image of cause and effect, does not take into account these subtler aspects of thought's activity. This leads to what Bohm calls a 'systemic fault' in the whole of thought. The issue here, says Bohm, is that 'thought doesn't know it is doing something and then struggles against what it is doing'. For example, flattery is a pleasing experience which usually sets up a reflex of receptivity toward the one who flatters. If Jane fails to flatter John when he expects her to, or takes advantage of him in some unpleasant way, John will attribute his subsequent bad feelings to something Jane did. He fails to see that he participated in constructing the reflex that produced not only the good feelings, but the bad ones as well. A similar process of incoherence is at work in the nation-state. When the United States attributes diabolical characteristics to various Middle East countries that thwart its easy access to oil, it is not taking into account its own central involvement in an international petroleum-based economy which quite naturally gives inordinate power to those who possess crude oil. In this case, the reflexive response may be war. The feature common to both examples is the sense of being in control with an independent response: 'I will get even with her' or 'we must demonstrate where the real power lies'. In Bohm's view, the real power is in the activity of thought. While independence and choice appear to be inherent in our actions, we are actually being driven by agendas which act faster than, and independent of, our conscious choice. Bohm sees the pervasive tendency of thought to struggle against its own creations as the central dilemma of our time. Consequently, we must now endeavour not only to *apply* thought, but to understand what thought *is*, to grasp the significance of its immediate activity, both in and around us.

Is it possible, then, to be aware of the activity of thought without acquiring a new agenda, namely, the intention to 'fix' thought? Can we suspend our habit of defining and solving problems, and attend to thought as if for the first time? Such open learning, says Bohm, lays the foundation for an exploration of *proprioception*. Proprioception (literally, 'self-perception') is that which enables us to walk, sit, eat, or engage in any other daily activity without having constantly to monitor what we are doing. An instantaneous feedback system informs the body, allowing it to act without conscious control. If we wish to scratch a mosquito bite on the back of our leg, it is proprioception that allows us to scratch the bite without (a) looking at our hand, (b) looking at our leg or (c) having the mistaken impression that someone else is scratching our leg.

Dr Bohm points out that while proprioception of the body comes naturally, we do not seem to have proprioception of thought. If, however, mind and matter are indeed a continuum, it is reasonable to explore the extension of physiological proprioception into the more subtle material activity of thought. Bohm suggests that the immediacy and accuracy of bodily proprioception are inhibited at the level of thought due to the gross accumulation of reflexes, personified in the image of a 'thinker' – an interior entity who seems to look out on the world, as well as looking inwardly at emotions, thoughts and so on. This thinker, says Bohm, is a product of thought, rather than a transcendental entity; and the thinker is steadfastly committed to preserving some variation of its own reflexive structure. Here the state of open learning is crucial for new understanding. If the reflexive structure can be simply *attended to*, rather than *acted upon* (as the thinker would be inclined to do), then the momentum which drives the reflexes is already being dissipated. In this vein, Bohm outlines a series of practical experiments which call into awareness the interplay of words and feelings in the formation of reflexes. This conjunction of open learning and concrete experiments with the thought-feeling dynamic suggests the beginning of proprioception of thought.

Such proprioception is intimately related to that which Dr Bohm refers to as 'insight'. We often associate insight with the 'a-ha!' phenomenon of having suddenly grasped the significance of some puzzle or problem. Bohm's notion of insight includes such particular instances, but extends to a much more general, and generative, level of application. He sees insight as an *active energy*, a subtle level of intelligence in the universe at large, of a different order from that which we commonly experience in the mind/matter domain. He suggests that such insight has the capacity to directly affect the structure of the brain, dispelling the 'electrochemical fog' generated by accumulated reflexes. Quite unlike the memory-laden structure of a 'thinker' operating upon thought, proprioception provides a medium of appropriate subtlety for the activity of such insight. In this way, learning, proprioception and insight work together, with the potential to reorder our thought processes and bring about a general level of coherence unavailable through thought alone.

While all these experiments can be undertaken by individuals, Bohm points to a complementary mode of inquiry through the process of group *dialogue*. He suggests that such meetings have no advance agenda, other than the intention to explore thought. And though a facilitator may be useful in the beginning, the meetings should be free of authority so that people speak directly to one another. In groups of twenty to forty people, the systemic and reflexive nature of thought can come clearly into focus, eliciting a wide range of responses from the participants. Self-images, assumptions and prejudices may all emerge, often with their attendant emotions – defensiveness, anger, fear and many others. The virtue of such an approach, says Bohm, is that the group may be able to detect the *flow of meaning* passing amongst its members. This meaning may be the content of some particular subject; it may also be the quickened pulses that pass through the group as the result of conflict between two or more members. Such dialogue holds out the possibility of direct insight into the *collective* movement of thought, rather than its expression in any particular individual. Bohm suggests that the potential for collective intelligence inherent in such groups could lead to a new and creative art form, one which may involve significant numbers of people and beneficially affect the trajectory of our current civilization.

Throughout *Thought as a System* Dr Bohm emphasizes that the model of thought he puts forward is propositional. Not only does he deny any final knowledge of these issues for himself; he claims that no such knowledge is even possible. Such knowledge would be thought, which can only make approximate representations. Dr Bohm often invoked Alfred Korzybski's observation that any object of thought (including, for Bohm, thought itself) is both 'more than what we think, and different'. None the less, as we do rely to a great extent on images and representations, a relatively accurate map of the processes of thought, based on clear observation and sound inferences, is surely more desirable than a flawed map. It was Dr Bohm's intention that *Thought as a System* be approached as just such a propositional map, to be tested against direct life experiences, and measured by its veracity and its usefulness in reducing conflict and sorrow in the world at large.

Lee Nichol
Ojai, California
September, 1993

ACKNOWLEDGEMENTS

Since 1986 David Bohm went to Ojai, California, each year to give what came to be known as the David Bohm Seminars. These seminars were arranged by a small group of people without whom this book could not have been written, for it is an account of the 1990 seminar. David valued their help and friendship very much and I want to thank them on his behalf. They are Michael Frederick, Booth Harris, David Moody, Lee Nichol and Joe Zorskie. Also, a special thanks to Phildea Fleming and James Brodsky who transcribed, edited and printed these transcripts making them available to all who took part in the seminars. They were in constant telephone contact with David, going into all aspects of the editing of the audio-tapes and making it possible for him then to do the final editing.

None of this would have happened without all the participants to the seminars who became our friends over the years and the many other people involved. My thanks to them too. I would also like to thank the Directors and Board of the Oak Grove School in Ojai. The library there made the ideal setting for the seminars.

Lastly, I want to thank David Stonestreet of Routledge for his constant active interest in David Bohm's work and his unfailing help to me.

Sarah Bohm

FRIDAY EVENING

David Bohm: We have more people at this seminar than we've had before, a number of whom are here for the first time. I'll try not to be too repetitious, but we must go over some of the old ground. And we hope there will be some new material.

These meetings have been concerned with the question of *thought* and what it has been doing in the world.

By way of review, we all know that the world is in a difficult situation and has been basically for a long time; that we now have many crises in various parts of the world. We have the fact that there is nationalism all over. People seem to have all sorts of hatreds, such as religious hatred or racial hatred, and so on. There is the ecological crisis, which goes on and off the back burner, and there is the continuing economic crisis developing. People seem unable to get together to face the common problems, such as the ecological one or the economic one. Everything is interdependent; and yet the more interdependent we get, the more we seem to split up into little groups that don't like each other and are inclined to fight each other and kill each other, or at least not to cooperate.

So one begins to wonder what is going to happen to the human race. Technology keeps on advancing with greater and greater power, either for good or for destruction. And it seems that there is always this danger of destruction. No sooner does the rivalry between the West and the East sort

1

of dissolve away than other conflicts pop up elsewhere. And doubtless others will come up later, and on it goes. It's sort of endemic; it's not just something that occasionally happens. It's in the whole situation.

I think we are all familiar with this situation. And with technology advancing you have the possibility that nuclear bombs will perhaps soon be available to all sorts of dictators, even in relatively small nations. There are biological weapons and chemical weapons, and other kinds of weapons that haven't yet been invented but surely will. And then there is the economy to consider. Either we go into a depression, which will help save the ecology, or we go into a boom, which will momentarily make us happy but will eventually ruin the ecology. I mean, the faster we go into prosperity, the faster we create all of these other problems.

It seems that whichever way you turn, it doesn't really work. Why not? Is there any way out? Can you imagine that a hundred or two hundred or five hundred years of this won't lead to some gigantic catastrophe, either to the ecology or in some other way? Perhaps more wars, who knows?

People have been dealing with this piecemeal – looking at symptoms, saying that we've got to solve this problem or that problem or that problem. But there is something deeper, which people haven't been considering, that is constantly generating these problems. We can use the analogy of a stream, where people are pouring pollution upstream at the same time they are trying to remove it downstream. But as they remove it they may be adding more pollution of a different kind.

What is the source of all this trouble? That is really what we have been concerned with in all these dialogues of the past few years. I'm saying that the source is basically in thought. Many people would think that such a statement is crazy, because thought is the one thing we have with which to solve our problems. That's part of our tradition. Yet it looks as if the thing we use to solve our problems is the source of our problems. It's like going to the doctor and having him make you ill. In fact, in 20 per cent of medical cases we do apparently have that going on. But in the case of thought, it's far over 20 per cent.

I'm saying the reason we don't see the source of our problems is that the means by which we try to solve them are the source. That may seem strange to somebody who hears it for the first time, because our whole culture prides itself on thought as its highest achievement. I'm not suggesting that the achievements of thought are negligible; there are very great achievements in technology, in culture and in various other ways. But there is another side to it which is leading to our destruction, and we have to look at that.

Now I'll try to say what is wrong with thought. I'll just give a brief summary and then we might start talking about it, if you like.

One of the obvious things wrong with thought is *fragmentation*. Thought is breaking things up into bits which should not be broken up. We can see this going on. We see that the world is broken up into nations – more and more nations. Russia no sooner got rid of the communist dictatorship than it began breaking up into a lot of little bits which obviously are unable to manage, and they started fighting each other. That's a source of concern. It's a concern for the whole world. There are new nations all over the world. During the second World War, nationalism developed in Latvia, Lithuania and Estonia. They said 'Lithuania for the Lithuanians, Latvia for the Latvians, Armenia for the Armenians', and so on.

Nationalism has broken things up, and yet the world is all one. The more technology develops, the more people depend on each other. But people try to pretend that it's not so. They say that the nation is sovereign, that it can do what it likes. And yet it can't. The United States can't do what it likes because it depends a lot on other countries for things of all sorts – on the Middle East for oil, apparently on Japan for money. And Japan obviously can't do what it likes. Those are just some examples.

It seems very hard for human beings to accept seriously this simple fact of the effect of fragmentation. Nations fight each other and people kill each other. You are told that for

3

the nation you must sacrifice everything. Or you sacrifice everything for your religious differences. People split into religious groups. They split into racial groups and say that's all important. Inside each nation there are various splits. People are divided up into sections and into all kinds of interests. The division goes on down to the level of the family, inside families and so forth. People are supposed to be getting together, but they can't seem to.

You can see that nations are established by thought. The boundary of the nation is invented by thought. If you go to the edge of the nation, there's nothing to tell you that it is a boundary, unless somebody makes a wall or something. It's the same land; the people may often be not very different. But what is one side or the other seems all important. It's thought that 'makes it so'.

I was informed that most of the nations of the Middle East were invented either by the British or the French, whose various bureaucrats drew lines and determined the boundary of this nation, that nation, that nation. And there they were. So then they have to fight each other.

In other words, what we are doing is establishing boundaries where really there is a close connection – that's what is wrong with fragmentation. And at the same time we are trying to establish unity where there isn't any, or not very much. We say we're all one inside the boundary. But when you look at these groups, they are not actually all one. They are fighting each other inside the boundary as much as they are fighting outside.

We can also consider professional groups. In science, for instance, every little speciality is fragmented from every other one. People hardly know what is happening in a somewhat different field. And it goes on. Knowledge is fragmented. Everything gets broken up.

Thus we have false division and false unification. Thought is pretending that there is a sharp division outside and that everything is unified inside, when it's really not so. This is a fictional way of thinking. But to go on with this fictional way of thinking seems to be very important, so important that the actual fact that it is wrong, the fact that it's not that way at all, is ignored.

It seems strange. Why should people do such a strange thing? It really could be thought of as irrational at the very least, or perhaps crazy. So much trouble, which may even prevent our survival, is created out of such small things.

The more general difficulty with thought is that thought is very active, it's *participatory*. And fragmentation is itself a symptom of the more general difficulty. Thought is always doing a great deal, but it tends to say that it hasn't done anything, that it is just telling you the way things are. But thought affects everything. It has created everything we see in this building. It has affected all the trees, it has affected the mountains, the plains and the farms and the factories and science and technology. Even the South Pole has been affected because of the destruction of the ozone layer, which is basically due to thought. People thought that they wanted to have refrigerant – a nice safe refrigerant – and they built that all up by thinking more and more about it. And now we have the ozone layer being destroyed.

Thought has produced tremendous effects outwardly. And, as we'll discuss further on, it produces tremendous effects inwardly in each person. Yet the general tacit assumption in thought is that it's just telling you the way things are and that is not doing anything – that 'you' are inside there, deciding what to do with the information. But I want to say that you don't decide what to do with the information. The information takes over. *It* runs *you*. Thought runs you. Thought, however, gives the false information that you are running it, that you are the one who controls thought, whereas actually thought is the one which controls each one of us. Until thought is understood – better yet, more than understood, *perceived* – it will actually control us; but it will create the impression that it is our servant, that it is just doing what we want it to do.

That's the difficulty. Thought is participating and then saying it's not participating. But it is taking part in everything.

5

Fragmentation is a particular case of that. Thought is creating divisions out of itself and then saying that they are there naturally. The divisions between nations are regarded as being 'just there', but obviously they were invented by people. People have come to accept those divisions and that made them be there. The same holds for the divisions between religions. Every religion was invented by somebody's thinking that he had a certain idea about God that was right and true. Eventually people thought that other religions weren't right, that other religions were inferior, perhaps even heretical or evil or wrong, that they could fight them, try to suppress them and destroy them. There were vast religious wars. And we may still have more coming, in spite of all the development of the enlightenment, knowledge and science and technology. In fact, science and technology now seem, at least equally well, to serve those who are perhaps at a more Mediaeval stage as it serves those who regard themselves as more advanced. Anybody can use science and technology without fundamentally altering his own frame of mind which governs how they are used.

I'm saying thought has the character that it is doing something and saying it isn't doing it. Now, we really have to go into that, to discuss it a great deal, because what thought is actually doing is very much more subtle than what I've described – that's only the beginning.

Another problem of fragmentation is that thought divides itself from feeling and from the body. Thought is said to be the mind; we have the notion that it is something abstract or spiritual or immaterial. Then there is the body, which is very physical. And we have emotions, which are perhaps somewhere in between. The idea is that they are all different. That is, we *think* of them as different. And we experience them as different because we think of them as different.

But thought is not different from emotion. We'll discuss this in more detail later; but for a very elementary example, if you think that a certain person has treated you badly you may get angry. Suppose that somebody keeps you waiting for a couple of hours. You can get angry thinking: 'What does he mean treating me like this? He has no concern, no consideration for me.' You can think of various things: 'He's always doing this, he treats me badly', and so on. By thinking that way you can get very angry. Then if he comes and explains that the train was late, the anger goes. This shows that the emotion was influenced by thought. By changing your thought, the anger fades.

So thought at least can sustain those feelings. The thought of something pleasant will make you feel good. The thought that you are doing great will make you feel good inside – all the good feelings will come out. Or the thought that you have done something wrong may make the adrenalin flow, may make you feel guilty. If somebody says you are guilty, which is a thought, then you can feel very miserable. Feelings are tremendously affected by thoughts. And obviously thoughts are tremendously affected by feelings, because if you are angry you don't think clearly. Likewise, if you have a feeling of pleasure in something you may find yourself reluctant to give up that idea which gives you pleasure, even if it is wrong – you engage in self-deception.

There's a good physical reason that feelings and thoughts affect each other; you can see it in the structure of the brain. There is an intellectual centre in the cortex, the outer layers of the brain. And deeper down there is an emotional centre. Between them is a very thick bundle of nerves, by which they communicate very closely. So they are connected. There was a famous case in the nineteenth century of a man who had an iron pin driven through his brain by an explosion. He apparently recovered from this, and he was physically more or less normal. But although he had been a very level-headed man, after he recovered he was totally unbalanced emotionally, and intellectually he couldn't maintain any very consistent line of thought. The breaking of the connection between the emotional and the intellectual centres prevented the system from functioning.

The intellectual centre will normally tell whether an emotion is appropriate or not. That is what happens in the example of being angry about somebody's delaying you two

7

hours, and then coming along and saying 'The train was late.' If you believe him, then the intellectual centre says 'there's no longer any good reason to be angry'. And the emotional centre duly says 'OK, no reason, I give up my anger'. And vice versa – the emotional centre may send information saying that there is danger, or there is this or that, and the intellectual centre picks it up and tries to find out what is the danger. It *thinks*.

Those centres are intimately and closely related. The very wish to think must come from an emotion or from an impulse to think. They are really almost two sides of the same process. But our language separates them and our thought separates them into fragments. I'm saying that emotion and intellect are closely connected, but we introduce into our thought a very sharp division – just like the one between nations – where there really isn't such a division. We're introducing a fictional way of thinking about this situation. If our thinking is fictional, it will mislead us.

It is worth repeating what I've said the last few years – that in our language we have a distinction between 'thinking' and 'thought'. 'Thinking' implies the present tense – some activity going on which may include critical sensitivity to what can go wrong. Also there may be new ideas, and per-haps occasionally perception of some kind inside. 'Thought' is the past participle of that. We have the idea that after we have been thinking something, it just evaporates. But thinking doesn't disappear. It goes somehow into the brain and leaves something – a trace – which becomes thought. And thought then acts automatically. The example I gave about the person who kept you waiting shows how thought reinforces and sustains anger; when you have been thinking for a while, 'I have a good reason to be angry', the emotion is there and you remain angry. So thought is the response from memory – from the past, from what has been done. Thus we have thinking and thought.

We also have the word 'feeling'. Its present tense suggests the active present, that the feeling is directly in contact with reality. But it might be useful to introduce the word *'felt'*, to say there are feelings and 'felts'. That is, 'felts' are feelings which have been recorded. You may remember pleasure that you once had, and then you get a sense of pleasure. If you remember pain you had you may get a sense of pain. A traumatic experience in the past can make you feel very uncomfortable when remembered. Nostalgic feelings are also from the past. A lot of the feelings that come up are really from the past, they're 'felts'. By failing to make this distinction we often give too much importance to some feelings which actually don't have that much significance. If they are just a recording being replayed, they don't have as much significance as if they were a response to the present immediate situation.

Often you may respond according to the way you felt a long time ago, or the way you became used to feeling in the past. In effect you could be saying 'when I was a child, a certain situation made me feel uncomfortable', and then when any similar situation arises in the present you feel uncomfortable. You get that discomfort because you don't see that it doesn't mean anything. But it does seem to mean a great deal, and it affects you.

So not only is there a false division between thinking and feeling, but also between feelings and 'felts', and the whole state of the body. You can see that the way you think can get adrenalin flowing. You can get neurochemically affected all over the body. For example, if you are in an area which you think is dangerous and you see a shadow, your thought says that there are people around who might attack you, and then you immediately get a feeling of fear. Your adrenalin starts flowing, your muscles tense, your heart beats rapidly – just from the knowledge that there may be assailants in the neighbourhood. As soon as you look and say 'it's a shadow', those physical symptoms subside. There is a profound connection between the state of the body and the way you think. If people are constantly worried and under stress about their jobs or something, they may stir up their stomachs too much and get ulcers and various other things. It's well known. The state of the body is very profoundly tied to thought, affected by thought, and vice versa. That's another kind of fragmentation we have to watch out for.

All of this will tend to introduce quite a bit of confusion, or what I call 'incoherence', into thinking or into action because you will not get the results you expect. That's the major sign of incoherence: you want to do something but it doesn't come out the way you intend. That's usually a sign that you have some wrong information somewhere. The right approach would be to say; 'Yes, that's incoherent. Let me try to find out the wrong information and change it.' But the trouble is, there is a lot of incoherence in which people don't do that.

For instance, perhaps somebody likes to be flattered and he then finds that the person who flatters him can take advantage of him. It happens again and again and again. He doesn't want that, but it happens. There is an incoherence there because it's not his intention to be taken advantage of. But he has another intention he doesn't think about, which is that he wants the glow of feeling that comes from the flattery. You can see that one implies the other, because if he accepts the flattery then he also will accept a lot of other things the person says or does. He can be taken advantage of. Therefore, he has both a conscious intention, and another one which is going against it. That's a very common situation.

It is the same with nationalism. People didn't set up nations in order to suffer the way they've suffered – to suffer endless wars and hate and starvation and disease and annihilation and slavery and whatnot. When they set up the nations it was not their intention to do that. But that's what has happened. And it would inevitably happen. The point is that people rarely look at the nation and ask, 'what's it all about?' Rather, they say 'at all costs we've got to go on with this nation, but we don't want these consequences'. And they struggle against the consequences while they keep on producing the situation.

This is another major feature of thought: *thought doesn't know it is doing something and then it struggles against what it is doing*. It doesn't want to know that it is doing it. And it struggles against the results, trying to avoid those unpleasant results while keeping on with that way of thinking. That is what I call *sustained* incoherence. There is also *simple* incoherence, which we can't avoid having because thoughts are always incomplete – thought can never be complete, as we'll discuss later. But when we find that what is happening is contradictory or confused or isn't doing what we expect, then we should change our thoughts to reflect what is happening. And in simple situations we do. When it comes to things that matter to us, though, it seems we generally don't. Now this is rather odd, because the things that matter are where we ought to be especially coherent. However, we feel we can afford to be coherent only in the things that don't matter too much – which is another kind of incoherence.

Nobody has the intention of producing this sort of situation. We are producing these situations contrary to our conscious intentions because there is another resistance going on of which we're not very conscious. So whenever we intend to do something we often unconsciously have a resistance trying to prevent us from doing it. That's obviously a big waste of energy, and it is very destructive. It means we will produce problems without end which have no solution.

In the recent past the East and the West have got together for various reasons. But for various other reasons, people were sending a lot of arms into the Middle East over the years. It was not their intention to produce an impossible situation with Iraq. They said; 'Well, we're sending arms to the Middle East. We want to make money. We have a certain national policy to maintain. There are many reasons.' And then it all added up to a very dangerous situation. If there had been no arms sent there, it would not have been so serious. Also, in 1973 it was plainly brought out that the West is very dependent on oil from the Middle East, which is a very unstable region. For a while people began to use their oil and their energy more efficiently. Gradually they became less concerned with doing so. And then later they say; 'Look!

11

Surprise. We now depend on them. Half of the oil of the world is theirs. If that goes we're all finished.'

Clearly it is not people's intention to produce these situations. Rather, they may say, 'we don't want this situation, but there are a lot of other things we've got to have'. But those things will produce these situations. There's an incoherence there.

We are constantly producing situations and things which we don't intend and then we say 'look, we've got a problem'. We don't realize that it is our deeper, hidden intentions which have produced it, and consequently we keep on perpetuating the problem. Even now very little is being done, as far as I can see, about using energy more efficiently and thus becoming less dependent on Middle Eastern oil – which would remove much of the whole problem.

So we must ask 'why do we have this incoherence?' Nobody wants these situations, and yet the things people think they want will inevitably produce them. It is thought that makes people say 'that's necessary'. Therefore, thought has come to this kind of incoherence.

Now, that is really a kind of introduction. Maybe we should talk a little about it for a while.

Questioner: I'm unclear on the point about the difference between thinking and thought. Are you proposing that we slide from thinking into thought without being aware that we are doing it?

Bohm: Yes. It's automatic, because when we've been thinking, that thinking gets recorded in the brain and becomes thought. I'll discuss later how that thought is an active set of movements, a *reflex*. But suppose you keep telling very young children that people of a certain group are no good, no good, no good. Then later on it becomes thought which just springs up – 'they're no good'. In fact, you hardly notice that you are thinking, that there is any thought even.

Q: Right now, in conversation with this group, while you're talking there's a process of thinking which is, as you explained, more alive in the present. And then this other stuff is happening, which is thought. We don't seem to have the ability to distinguish the two.

Bohm: No, we don't seem to distinguish the two. Sometimes we do though, because sometimes we say, 'I thought that before'. But generally we may miss the distinction. And with feeling it's even harder to see that distinction between the past feeling coming up – I call it the 'felt' – and something which would be an active present feeling.

Q: I wonder how much of the fracturing is taught in the Newtonian and Christian models. Is this actually the brain's behaviour, its normal natural behaviour? I remember in grade schools being taught to fracture, classify and disorganize, to take things apart. And my interior was violently against it because I saw this whole knotted skein as an uneducated person. So I'm wondering whether the brain naturally wants to fracture and analyse, or is it part of the way we teach ourselves?

Bohm: It is to some extent partly the result of the way we are taught. But I think there is some tendency in thought to build this up constantly.

Q: Do you think it is partly intrinsic in the nature of the brain?

Bohm: Not of the brain, but of the way thought has developed. A certain amount of analysis is necessary for clarity of thought; some distinctions have to be made. But we carry them too far without knowing. We slip over. And

13

once we carry them too far, then we start assuming they are just 'what is', and that becomes part of our habit.

Q: How do we recognize where the edge is, before slipping over too far?

Bohm: That's a very subtle question, and we want to go into that carefully during this whole seminar. To get free of that is much more than just recognizing that difference. Something much deeper is involved. What we have to do first is to get some notion of what sort of trouble we're in now.

We started out saying the trouble is that the world is in chaos, but I think we end up by saying that *thought* is in chaos. That's each one of us. And that is the cause of the world's being in chaos. Then the chaos of the world comes back and adds to the chaos of thought.

Q: Are you saying that thought has a kind of possessive quality which stays, gets stuck, and then becomes habitual? And we don't see this?

Bohm: I think that whenever we repeat something it gradually becomes a habit, and we get less and less aware of it. If you brush your teeth every morning, you probably hardly notice how you're doing it. It just goes by itself. Our thought does the same thing, and so do our feelings. That's a key point.

Q: Isn't the employment of thought in the psychological sense synonymous with corruption?

Bohm: Why do you say that?

Q: Are there not only two states: corruption and innocence?

Bohm: Are you saying that thought by itself is incapable of innocence?

Q: In the psychological sense it seems so.

Bohm: It may seem so. But the question is whether it is actually so. That's the question we're trying to explore. We'll admit the fact that it seems so; it has that appearance. Now the question is: what is actually the case? We have to explore this, and it will take some digging into. We can't simply take the way things seem and just work on that, because that would be another kind of mistake thought makes – taking the surface and calling it the reality.

Q: I think what you said is really interesting. I see that if I have the intention to go somewhere but take the wrong road, it's no problem. The next time I find out what the right road is, change the information, and take a different road. But I often have the intention to do something personally and collectively and it doesn't work out. Yet I don't know what's wrong. I can't seem to change the information.

What I'm especially interested in is how there's a sense of 'me' separate from the information and from the intention. I feel as though I'm the subjective being who can change it, and yet I can't seem to; or the world can't seem to. This sense of 'me' separate from the information – would that be something interesting to explore?

Bohm: That's another subtle question, and we will try to get into it during this whole period.

We have that feeling, as you say. But we shouldn't necessarily accept what seems to be. If we accept 'what seems to be' as 'what is', then we can't inquire. I mean, if what seems to be were perfectly coherent, then I'd say 'all right, why question it?' But since it is highly incoherent, I would say there is a good reason to question it. That would be common

15

sense in ordinary areas of life. It does seem that all that is happening – we all want to do things and we can't do what we want. Something else seems to happen which stops us.

Some of the people who are running corporations are getting interested in this question because they have the same problem. I know some people who are working in this area, and they find that when their boards get together they can't seem to agree and they can't get the results they intend. That's one of the reasons they are sinking a bit.

A fellow named Peter Senge has written a book called *The Fifth Discipline*. He has analysed some of these questions. I don't say that he's got to the bottom of it, but it's interesting. His analysis shows that very often there are problems because people are not following the effect of their thoughts – that when they think something and something is done, it then spreads out to other companies, and then it comes back a bit later as if it were something else independent. They treat it as an independent problem and they keep on, thereby making it worse because they keep on doing the same thing. So their way of thinking is creating a problem. It takes some time for the problem to get back to them; and by that time they've lost track of it and they say 'here's a problem'. Then they think some more and produce more of that problem, or else change the problem a bit into another one that's worse, or whatever. The point is that they are not following the effects of their thought. They are not aware of the fact that thought is active and participating.

When you are thinking something, you have the feeling that the thoughts do nothing except inform you the way things are and then *you* choose to do something and you do it. That's what people generally assume. But actually, the way you think determines the way you're going to do things. Then you don't notice a result comes back, or you don't see it as a result of what you've done, or even less do you see it as a result of how you were thinking. Is that clear?

So all these problems that I've described – that whole depressing series of them – are the result of the way we've been thinking. But people don't see that. They say, 'We're just thinking. Out there are the problems. The thinking is telling us about those problems – what they are.'

Q: Suppose I see a situation in which it seems so very obvious that a whole group of people are acting very incoherently. I think I see very clearly that they're being incoherent, and then I start to act to correct that. But if I'm not noticing that my own thinking may be incoherent, then my action won't be coherent.

Bohm: You may be caught in the same thing. And even if not, how will you actually correct it? Unless their thinking changes their action won't be corrected. Now, nothing you do can change their thinking, except communication to them that they're incoherent – communication which they will accept and understand. Otherwise you are trying to meet thought with force, which is really a kind of violence. If you say 'out there are some people behaving incoherently and I will try to make them behave coherently', then you're using force. But they keep on thinking the same old way. If you're more powerful than they are, they will do what you want for a while – until you get to be a little weak, and then they'll get back at you.

Q: I would like to explore this: thought comes in from the outside, comes into our awareness, takes over, takes possession – and maybe collectively takes possession and we go to war. But we don't see this because thought is possessive, like magic. It takes over.

Bohm: Yes, it takes over. And why does it take over? There are two levels of this point. One is to describe what happens as far as we can see outwardly. The second is to see the source of it, because unless we see the source it will never change.

17

Q: How can we explore the source?

Bohm: Well, that's what this weekend is about. But I think it's important to see what the question is. The first thing is to see that there is a question which needs to be explored.

Q: Can thought be aware of itself?

Bohm: That's also a subtle question. On the surface it appears that thought would not be aware of itself, if thought is just memory.

Let's say, however, that we need some kind of awareness of what thought is doing – that seems clear – but which we don't have, generally speaking. I've used the word 'proprioception' in previous seminars to mean 'self-perception of thought', and we'll come to that as we go along. It may be that thought can be aware of itself. But it would take us rather longer than we have to get into that this evening, so for the present I think we should look at the thing in sort of a general way.

It doesn't look entirely impossible that we could approach this question somehow, but it is a very difficult question. I would suggest that one reason why it is difficult is that there is a *fault* in the process of thought.

What I mean by 'thought' is the whole thing – thought, 'felt', the body, the whole society sharing thoughts – it's all one process. It is essential for me not to break that up, because it's all one process; somebody else's thoughts become my thoughts, and vice versa. Therefore it would be wrong and misleading to break it up into my thought, your thought, my feelings, these feelings, those feelings. For some purposes that's all right, but not for the purpose we're talking about now.

I would say that thought makes what is often called in modern language a *system*. A system means a set of connected things or parts. But the way people commonly use the word nowadays it means something all of whose parts are mutually interdependent – not only for their mutual action, but for their meaning and for their existence.

A corporation is organized as a system – it has this department, that department, that department. They don't have any meaning separately; they only can function together. And also the body is a system. Society is a system in some sense. And so on.

Similarly, thought is a system. That system not only includes thoughts, 'felts' and feelings, but it includes the state of the body; it includes the whole of society – as thought is passing back and forth between people in a process by which thought evolved from ancient times.

A system is constantly engaged in a process of development, change, evolution and structure changes, and so forth, although there are certain features of the system which become relatively fixed. We call this the *structure*. You can see that in an organization there's a certain structure. Then sometimes that structure begins to break up because it doesn't work, and people may have to change it.

We have some structure in thought as well – some relatively fixed features. Thought has been constantly evolving and we can't say when that structure began. But with the growth of civilization it has developed a great deal. It was probably very simple thought before civilization, and now it has become very complex and ramified and has much more incoherence than before.

So we have this system of thought. Now, I say that this system has a fault in it – a *systemic fault*. It's not a fault here, there or there, but it is a fault that is all throughout the system. Can you picture that? It's everywhere and nowhere. You may say 'I see a problem here, so I will bring my thought to bear on this problem'. But 'my' thought is part of the system. It has the same fault as the fault I'm trying to look at, or a similar fault.

We have this systemic fault; and you can see that this is what has been going on in all these problems of the world – such as the problems that the fragmentation of nations has

19

produced. We say: 'Here is a fault. Something has gone wrong.' But in dealing with it, we use the same kind of fragmentary thought that produced the problem, just a somewhat different version of it; therefore it's not going to help, and it may make things worse. You may say that you see all these things going on and then ask 'what shall I do?' You try to think about it, but by now your thought is pervaded by this systemic fault. Then what does that call for?

Q: Is it that the whole system has been polluted?

Bohm: That's one way of looking at it, yes. Something has happened in the entire system which makes the thought wrong – the whole process in the system is not straight. There may be bits which are all right, but it doesn't stay. It's somewhat like the way they used to talk of an egg which was rotten only in parts. There might be some parts which haven't gone rotten, but the rot will spread.

We can get some relatively clear thought in science. But even there it is not entirely clear because scientists are worried about their prestige and status, and so on. Sometimes they won't consider ideas that don't go along with their theories or with their prejudices. Nevertheless, science is aimed at seeing the fact, whether the scientist likes what he sees or not – looking at theories objectively, calmly, and without bias. To some extent, relatively coherent thought has been achieved better in science than in some other areas of life. Some results flowed out of science and technology which are quite impressive – a great power was released.

But now we discover that whenever the time comes to *use* science we just forget the scientific method. We just say that the use of what scientists have discovered will be determined by the needs of our country, or by my need to make money, or by my need to defeat that religion or merely by my need to show what a great powerful person I am. So we see that relatively unpolluted thought has been used to develop certain things, and then we always trust to the most polluted thought to decide what to do with them. That's part of the incoherence.

Q: Are you saying that we are in this pollution and we can't see our true intentions?

Bohm: We don't see that our intentions are incoherent – that perhaps they are arising out of the pollution.

Q: I think as individuals we strive to resolve these things in ourselves – what are our intentions as individuals? What causes us to act the way we do? And at the same time I see that part of the global problems you described are a different kind of problem which individuals haven't faced. For example, individuals want to survive and want to reproduce. That's no longer possible in the sense that it was in the past, because a lot of our problems are due to having too many people. We're supposed to be working on this as individuals and somehow collectively realizing that we can't do the same basic things individuals used to need to do, realizing that something has to be changed.

Bohm: Yes, that's quite true, but we can't seem to do it. People trying to get together to deal with these things don't seem to be able to get very far. Take the ecological pollution or the change of climate. Very little has been done to deal with those problems. A lot of good words have been produced by various governments, but when it comes to putting a lot of money behind their words they haven't gone very far. Those very good intentions are counteracted by another set of intentions, or a whole bunch of sets of intentions – such as we can't interfere with this, or we can't interfere with that or we've got to allow this and that and the other. And then it all adds up to very little.

So it's the same incoherence. The intentions which we profess are blocked by another set that we not only don't profess but may not know fully that we have. We may not want to know.

Q: It seems we have to become aware of certain assumptions, which we aren't even aware we have. We need to question what assumptions in the system we are taking for granted and how we operate all the time, because there's something we're not noticing which is limiting our ability to make our intentions happen, both individually and collectively.

Bohm: I think that we're not really aware of what is happening in this system which I've called 'thought'. We don't know how it works. We hardly know it is a system; it's not part of our culture even to admit that it is a single system.

Q: Would you explain the system again? You said thought has a systemic flaw, but you're also including the emotions. What else are you including?

Bohm: The state of the body, the emotions, and also the whole society – the culture, the way we pass information between us, and so on.

Q: When you say 'the state of the body', are you also including the organs of the body?

Bohm: Yes, the organs are affected by it.

Q: Are you saying that the whole thing is a closed system?

Bohm: No, I wouldn't say it's entirely closed. A system isn't necessarily closed. It can be open to various influences of things coming in and out. That's the whole idea of a system. It's not necessarily closed, but it has a certain stability of structure. It tends to sustain and maintain its structure, so that when something from the outside comes in it reacts in such a way as to avoid basic change.

Q: But I'm hoping you're going to say that there is a possibility of opening up the structure, or seeing it.

Bohm: There is, yes. I'm not saying the system is everything there is. I'm saying that the system pervades our whole activity. It's like something pervading our activity; but that doesn't mean that it's all there is. Do you get the distinction? The system has become so pervasive, however, that it may be almost all that we are able to see much of the time.

Q: Can you say what is not part of the system?

Bohm: We could say for one thing, that perhaps there is some kind of perception or intelligence which is deeper, which is able to see this incoherence. The system itself could not see its incoherence very far, because it would distort it. But I'm suggesting that there is a capacity to see the incoherence.

As we've said, to a certain extent the system is necessary. We need this system of thought for all sorts of purposes. But it has developed a fault. Now there is, I say, an intelligence or a perception which goes beyond memory. There's a lot beyond this system. The system is actually only a very tiny part of reality; but it looms very large. Unless you actually *see* the thing I'm talking about, what I say will be incorporated into the system as an image. Is it clear what the problem is? This system tends to incorporate everything. Anything repeated several times becomes part of the system. Also somebody may have an insight and then that may easily become part of the system.

Q: Do you exclude intuition from the system?

23

Bohm: It depends on what you mean by 'intuition'. I think the system is able to imitate a kind of intuition. It may give a memory of intuition, which feels a bit like intuition.

Q: But intuition would not be part of the system, would it?

Bohm: Not if it were truly so. I'm saying there is 'perception' or 'insight' or 'intelligence' which may not be part of the system. There are various things you can call it, which we'll try to bring out as we go along. Whatever we call it, let's say for now that I don't think it is part of the system. That way we are keeping our possibilities open, and we may see some evidence that the system is not everything.

Q: Aren't there times an action takes place as a result of what you might call non-self-serving thought – not trying to impose it on someone – where there's a strong element of compassion and love in that particular thought? Then the fragmentation of thought is not really necessarily a part of that activity.

Bohm: If there were such compassion and love then I would say it's not part of the system, clearly. But, of course, a lot of what is felt to be compassion and love is actually part of the system, because once again such experiences, when repeated, become a habit. Thought can produce experiences without our being aware that they are produced by thought. It is this deceptive feature of thought that we have to watch out for. The worst confusion takes place in the question of what is *not* part of the system, because if you confuse part of the system as not being part of the system then you're lost. So you have to be very careful about that. It's no use just saying that love will take care of everything. People have said that for ages, but it hasn't done it. The Christian religion was based on the idea that God is love. They said that there is one God who is pure love, and Christ, and so on. Neverthe-

24

less, the Christians fought not only other religions but they also fought each other violently. They carried out very violent religious wars lasting centuries and did terrible things. Now I'm sure these people didn't intend to get into that; they had another intention. But because of the way they were thinking about their religion they couldn't help it. Theological ideas, for example, took over from ideas of love. Or there was a question of the religion being connected with the monarchy or power, or whatever. So violence doesn't stop merely by saying, 'we'll act based on love', because that can become just an idea that gets absorbed into the system.

Q: If all I've ever known in my whole life lies within the system, then any notion of there being anything outside of that is only a notion of the system. And I can't have any idea what that would mean.

Bohm: We don't know what it means, but we have to entertain the idea. I think we have to be careful not to paint ourselves into a corner here – to say that everything is in the system and there is no way out of it.

Q: I'm just saying I might get the notion that I could visualize something which was outside.

Bohm: That would still be inside. That becomes the most dangerous source of confusion, because then you say 'that's outside, it's all right'. In such a way thought produces something which seems to be outside, and it doesn't notice that it is doing so. That's one of the basic mistakes. Thought produces something and says, 'I didn't produce it. It's really there.'

Q: Are you saying that using thought to establish boundaries leads to fragmentation; rather we should see the difference between what is the system and what is not the system?

25

Bohm: If we *could* see it. But the question is how we are going to see it.

Q: There have been a lot of times when people have had insights into particular systems, or become aware of something and made a major change. There was a time before science became established when people believed in magic, and then came science. There are a lot of cases like that, where people did have a radical change in a limited sphere. I wonder if looking at how they did it in a particular area would be useful or relevant to getting to the root of this whole system.

Bohm: Do you have something in mind?

Q: Well for one thing, how did human beings manage to go from never having science to having science?

Bohm: That's an interesting point. How was it possible for scientific knowledge to develop which was quite contrary to the previous culture? That required what I like to call *insight*. I can give you several examples. From the time of the ancient Greeks up through the Middle Ages people believed that the earth was at the centre of the universe and that there were seven crystal spheres of increasing perfection. The seventh one was the perfect one. The basic idea was an order of increasing perfection, and the idea that each thing is striving to reach its right place. It was a highly organic view of the universe. Accordingly, they said: 'Celestial bodies, being perfect, should move in perfect figures. The only perfect figure is a circle, therefore those bodies ought to be moving in circles.' Then when they found that the planets didn't do so they tried to save the appearances, saying: 'well, it's not actually a circle, but we can make it up out of circles on top of circles – circles called epicycles.' That is, when they found

26

that the belief wasn't working too well they tended to move to save it rather than to question it seriously.

Gradually evidence accumulated, especially after the end of the Middle Ages, that there wasn't a great difference between heavenly and earthly matter. The moon, for instance, had a lot of irregular features on it; it wasn't very perfect. Not only the earth, but also other planets had satellites. And so on. There wasn't a lot of evidence that heavenly matter and earthly matter were all that different. But still the idea persisted that heavenly matter was basically different. 'It's heavenly, it's perfect, it belongs up there. It stays up there where it belongs.' And for a time, everybody was satisfied.

There was enough evidence by the time of Newton, or even before, to question that seriously, and some people may have done so. But there is sort of an unconscious level where it still works, saying: 'Why does the moon stay up in the sky? It's only natural. It's celestial matter, it stays up where it belongs.' Nobody worries about why it isn't falling. Now, that explanation may have made sense in ancient times, and there was an old habit in the mind not to question it – just to take it for granted. By the time of Newton, however, there was enough evidence to question it.

The story is, whether it's true or not I don't know, that Newton was watching an apple fall and had an insight. The question may have been in his mind, 'why isn't the moon falling?' And he suddenly had the answer: 'The moon *is* falling. That's the force of universal gravitation. Everything is falling towards every thing.' And then he had to explain why the moon doesn't reach the ground, which he was able to do later by some calculation showing that it was also going outward. Because it was far away it was moving away from the earth in a fast orbit that kept it off the ground while it was still falling.

So he must have had an insight at that moment, which broke that old mould of thought. Previously, nobody bothered with the question of why the moon wasn't falling, because it seemed so natural that the celestial matter stayed where it belonged. The key point of the insight was to break the

27

old mold of thought. From there on it was not very difficult to go to the new thought, because you could say that if the moon is falling then there is universal gravitation – everything is falling. And you could then go on from there.

There were other cases of that kind, and together they led to our more modern view. But now this more modern view is just as rigidly fixed as the ancient view was, and it would take something to break that too. People now tend to say that this is the absolute truth, final, no more really basic questions need to be asked that might perhaps throw some doubt on the whole framework underlying modern science – as happened with the older Greek and Mediaeval frameworks several centuries ago. Of course Newton's insight only broke the pattern in some limited domain. It didn't break the pattern in this vast area that we've been talking about. In other words, all these insights in science were ultimately assimilated within the general system of thought.

What I'm suggesting is that there is quite *general insight* that is possible which can break an old mode of thought. We'll come back to this again. We have to really look at it. We have to think about an area first, and then see what we can see. That opens the way to something else.

Q: When you say we have to think about it, isn't that the system doing the thinking?

Bohm: It may be or may not be. I think we shouldn't prejudge the issue. I'm saying it may be possible in a flash for some real thinking suddenly to take place. It must happen occasionally, or else where would we be? We would never have got anywhere at all. If we always used the kind of thought we use in nationalism to deal with practical problems we would have been dead long ago.

Q: Would it be correct to say that Newton's insight was seeing that the natural state of everything is not motionless?

Bohm: Yes. But even before the insight into gravitation there was already another insight, which was that the natural state of things is to be in motion, to which Galileo also contributed. I didn't give the full story of it. I focused on one point of gravitation.

Q: What you were saying is very interesting in that Newton was able to pose a question which he wasn't supposed to ask. And then the pattern of thinking was broken.

Bohm: Well, that can happen when people are generally asking wrong questions and then somebody comes along and asks a right question. A wrong question is one which already assumes the very thing that ought to be questioned. It's called 'begging the question'. Before Newton, people in physics were generally asking wrong questions because they were not aware of the importance of the question of why the moon isn't falling. They might have asked: 'Why is the moon going from here to there? Why is this planet going in this particular set of epicycles?', and so on. Those would have been wrong questions because they would have tacitly assumed that planets move in the sphere in which they belong. To do this was, of course, not relevant to the actual situation. So because they didn't question that whole structure, they may have been led to ask a lot of other questions which had no great meaning and thus get into deeper confusion. Your questions contain hidden assumptions; that's the point. Therefore, when you question the question itself, you may be questioning a deeper assumption. But that's done non-verbally. Do you see what I mean? To question the question eventually has to be a non-verbal act, which you can't describe.

Q: And that may break all the patterns?

Bohm: Yes, somehow it breaks the pattern.

Now, the suggestion is that this pattern of the system is not

29

something with which we are stuck. It may not be absolutely inevitable; there are signs that it could break.

Q: What do you mean when you say that questioning the question has to be non-verbal?

Bohm: If I say I have a question which may contain assumptions that should be questioned, I could question them verbally. But what would lead me to question my question? Eventually I can put it into words; but I'm saying the first step, the first flash of insight, is non-verbal.

Q: Are perceptions in the absence of thought, and then thought becomes a product of that?

Bohm: Yes, thought is affected by the perceptions. It takes a new turn by those perceptions.

Q: If insight isn't thought then what is it?

Bohm: We really have to go into that carefully. How would we answer that? Thought cannot adequately answer it. But then on the other hand, thought could still say something about it which might help us toward the question. We're not trying to say thought is always the culprit or always bad. It can also in many cases be right, not only technically but in other areas. However, I think that the kind of thought that would come in a thing like this, is a sudden feeling of waking up a bit.

Q: On the inside, is there an unlimited pool of insight with which any one of us could be in touch?

Bohm: Again, how would I answer that? I'm trying to say

'look at the question'. I'm saying that this is a matter of learning to question the question. Do you have an assumption that I could tell you 'yes' or 'no'? If I can't tell you, then what are we going to do?

Q: Look at the question.

Bohm: Yes. Don't answer it right away. Newton took a long time before he even got to the question, and he was quite bright.

Q: Can a perception take place that helps us to see how impatient we are; how thought likes to have answers and explanations too fast?

Bohm: We can look at that, too. Why do we want the answer right away?

Q: To get on with another question.

Bohm: Is that right? That means we're not interested in the question. If our real interest is to get on with another question, then we're not going to do this one very well.

Q: But that's what we do.

Q: Maybe it's like a computer, which wants to have information and conclusions right away. Maybe it's the nature of the machinery of thought.

Bohm: Well, that may be. But then we have to ask 'why do we allow ourselves to be subjugated by this machinery?'

31

Q: Could it be that getting an answer quickly makes us feel oriented and gives the sensation of security?

Bohm: But you could have said the same about Newton – that he may have wanted the answer right away. The question about the moon may have been disturbing. Even in science to raise fundamental questions can be very disturbing. Somebody could feel, 'I'd like to have the answer to this right away, and get out of this unpleasant state of disturbance', and he would never get anywhere.

Q: Generally it's uncomfortable not to know something.

Bohm: Yes. But then, Newton must have been in some state of not knowing. And I don't say only Newton; other scientists must have been for a period in some state of not knowing, or some state of confusion or incoherence or possibly some other unpleasant feelings. But I think Newton worked on it for quite a while. He must have gone through long periods which needn't have been always pleasant.

Q: Then to some extent we have to sustain the incoherence, not to get rid of it immediately?

Bohm: Yes, it's a mistake to think that you have got rid of the incoherence before you have in fact done so. Otherwise the system can create the appearance or the seeming of getting rid of it. The system seems to want to relive the pressure without actually getting to the root of the thing.

That's again the same problem, the same flaw, in another way – the same fault that we've been talking about. It's pervasive in the system. The system doesn't stay with the difficult problem that produces unpleasant feelings. It's conditioned somehow to move as fast as it can toward more pleasant feelings, without actually facing the thing that's making the unpleasant feeling.

Q: The thing about unpleasant feelings and confusion might be something that we learn. I've seen a child attempting to do some sort of puzzle, who tries without any sense of confusion or pain, just with interest – attempting again and again and again until maybe finally he succeeds. So does learning come out of a willingness to face something that does not have an immediate answer but is just sort of held in abeyance?

Bohm: That may well be, but we have to consider the state of the system which has evolved with our civilizations over thousands and thousands of years: we have a lot of bad experiences one way or another connected with not having the answers, and consequently there is a reaction immediately – we want the answer right away. It's the memory of all the unpleasant experiences of not having the answer. Those 'felts' bob up.

Q: Children are pushed to have the solution.

Bohm: They're rewarded if they have the right solution and they face a certain amount of unpleasantness if they don't have it. The educational system does that, the whole economic system does that, as does the political system. Everything has grown up to do that. By now that is part of this system of thought we've been discussing. Therefore, we have to say 'here we are in the system, and what are we going to do with it?' If we have unpleasantness, we might say; 'We shouldn't have it. It would be good not to have it.' But just saying this doesn't change anything. Rather we need to say; 'What are we going to do with it? What will be our response?'

Q: Can we get sensitivity to that here?

33

Bohm: We'll see if we can.

Q: It seems that it's not just an intellectual thing. Even listening to our voices here, there's a tone in the way we talk to each other which implies that what we are saying is literally so, rather than ideas or abstractions. And the child picks that up and it becomes 'I know. I know.'

Bohm: So can we face it here? Is there any unpleasantness in this group with regard to facing the uncertainty, or the unknown? You'll perhaps notice that there is a tremendous movement away. The system is set up to move away from awareness of that. Now, by inference – by just thinking about it clearly – we can see that it makes no sense to keep on doing that and the result must be real disaster. We could say 'my intention is not to do it'. But you will still find yourself doing it. You have a resistance coming from something else – from *the system*.

Q: Would part of the fault in the system be that we do not understand what is the role of incoherence in learning and in the system? We either try to get out of it immediately or else we stay in it indefinitely. We don't seem to find the golden means of the middle way, letting incoherence unfold itself sufficiently for us to understand what's going on.

Bohm: Sometimes we do. I think we understand perfectly well how that works because everybody does it in areas which are not too important to him.

Q: Then we need sensitivity to see what it means.

Bohm: Yes, but the system is *not* sensitive. The system interferes with sensitivity. It destroys it.

34

Q: I don't understand why we do not see the incoherence.

Bohm: Do we see it or don't we see it? It's a bit puzzling isn't it? Sometimes it seems we see it. In an elementary technical sense when somebody sees incoherence and it's not worrying him or frightening him he may actually learn from it, as was said. People do use incoherence. They begin to look at it if they're not too worried about it. But when people find that it's something important to them then they can't seem to do it.

Q: Is it that we have to re-educate our system – that when we're in a state of confusion or anxiety of not having an answer, we have to understand that there may be another possibility? It seems as though we have to actually articulate that possibility for the system, before even attempting to experience it.

Bohm: How would you do that?

Q: We have been educated to have an answer. All my life, as soon as the teacher asks a question, if I have the answer I'm a good kid. And then I hear for the first time that if I do not have the answer I'm a good kid. So the system is broadening to include something new which I never even conceived would be a possibility: it's OK to be confused, it might even be interesting. If I'm anxious it's usually hard for me not to want to find an answer, but hearing that anxiety is OK may in itself reduce the anxiety.

Bohm: That may help in some cases. But when you're really anxious – say if you have some situation involving real danger to you or your interest – I don't think it would always work. Nowadays people may be anxious about losing their jobs, for example, and they could become very anxious about that. It might help relax the mind a bit to think 'well, being anxious is all right'. But I'm not sure that many could sustain this for a long time if it proved to be necessary.

I would like to make this point: it's not merely that you have *heard* that this is all right, but you must have *seen* that it's all right. It would be still part of the system if you merely took my word that it is all right; unless, having actually heard it, you saw that it made sense.

Q: Are you saying we need to have a display?

Bohm: You have to *see* that it makes sense – that allowing anxiety to be there would be the coherent way to function or operate. If you're anxious you need to say: 'I'm anxious. That's part of the whole situation.' But then you have to notice that the system is conditioned to move away from that. And you have to be aware of that as well.

Therefore, by saying all this we have begun to move. By *seeing* it – seeing that it makes sense and is coherent – then a certain movement has begun, loosening up the system. So it shows that this system is not a monolithic rock wall; it's in fact not very solid at all, although it looks extremely solid.

Q: You're asking whether we can learn to become more learning-oriented individually and collectively, rather than 'I know' oriented?

Bohm: That's part of it. And another part is looking into impulses and feelings and anxieties which push us away from that. Instead of saying 'It's terrible, I'm anxious; I must quickly find some thought to relieve the anxiety', I now say 'Anxiety is perfectly normal and is to be expected in this situation'.

Q: It's an opportunity to learn.

Bohm: It's an opportunity to learn, yes. And this is a reversal of most of our culture.

Now, don't just accept this. If you see this makes sense and is coherent, that doesn't prove it is right but at least it suggests that it's a good approach.

Q: What you shunned before suddenly becomes valuable, at least as an opportunity.

Bohm: Yes. Krishnamurti used to use words like that, saying that envy or sorrow was a jewel. Then people would ask, 'How can he say such things? They're terrible things.' But the point is that if you look at it differently you can see that this is just what you've got to learn – what is actually going on, what it means. And the very fact that you have all this going on, which you don't really want, is a sign that there is incoherence.

Q: Do we attract to ourselves whatever we need to learn?

Bohm: Well, rather we acknowledge that things which we think we ought to get rid of are actually the clue to what we need to learn. Our whole culture and our whole instinct have told us that these are things we have to get rid of as quickly as we can. But now I've suggested reasons why maybe they are the source, the clue, for learning. In other words, from there we can begin to learn.

Q: And we never do learn because we don't look at them?

Bohm: That's one reason. There are probably a lot of other reasons. It is part of the system; our whole culture is part of the system, saying that we should get rid of pain or uncertainty as quickly as we can. And in addition, there is some instinctive tendency in that direction anyway – to get rid of whatever is painful.

That makes sense in certain areas, such as with a toothache. You have to deal with the tooth, to stop the pain. But even there it could be wrong. If your only intention was to get rid of the pain, you might just use various drugs to relieve the pain until the tooth decayed. If the pain is an indicator that something is wrong, it should be looked at in that way – something which is not coherent is going on.

It's very hard to get this straight, but the pain is in some way a sign, a result of a certain kind of incoherence. Biological pain may also very often be such a sign. In the tooth there is some bacterial process going on which is attacking the cells, and that is not coherent with the healthy operation of the body. Pain is a warning of that. So pain in general could be looked at that way.

There are people who cannot feel pain, and they really hurt themselves all the time. Their pain nerves are damaged. In fact, leprosy seems to be an instance of that. The pain nerves are damaged by the disease. It's an attack on the nerves, which prevents one from feeling pain, so that these people destroy their muscles by using too much force. It's been observed, watched carefully, that the destruction of leprosy comes from people using too much force in everything they do. They cannot tell how much force they are using, and they can be observed using fantastic amounts of force which destroy the whole system.

Thus, you can see that pain has a necessary function. And the instinctive wish to get rid of the pain – which works on the animal level – is not appropriate here with thought. That instinct is not good enough. Something much more deep and subtle is needed.

Q: Pain could also be a thought.

Bohm: Well, thought can be painful. The thought of what an

idiotic thing you've done, or what a fool you've made of yourself could be very painful.

Q: Or in other cases pain could be more like a perception, something not so much coming from thought.

Bohm: But even so, that pain is something to be perceived. Even if it comes from thought there is a perception needed in order to learn.

Q: The pain doesn't seem to come from thought though. The pain is something I generate in me in response to the thought.

Bohm: But it's part of the generalized thought, in the sense I'm using the word – of the whole bodily response.

Q: If I didn't understand that, I would try to use my thought to solve the problem of the pain which I am generating through my thinking. Whereas I am, in a sense, causing myself pain in response to the thought – unbeknownst to myself.

Bohm: Yes. You're hurting yourself; that is a simple way to put it.

Q: Once the thought or the image is there, isn't the response often immediate? I mean, it's not that we are doing it to ourselves so much as that the thought itself seems to bring physical pain.

Bohm: That's part of this generalized process. I'm trying to say that thought is never just thought, it's also the bodily state, the feeling, the nerves. Whatever is going on in the intellectual part connects with everything else. It flows out so fast that you can't keep it in one place. A thought of a certain kind will produce either pleasure or pain – or at least a memory of one of those feelings.

Q: Didn't you say that it's an immediate thing, that it is directly wired into the nervous system?

Bohm: Well, it could take a second or two before you feel the pain. It takes a second or two for the nerve impulses to get down to the solar plexus where you might feel the pain. And you don't realize that what you are feeling in the body has been stimulated by your thought, so you say 'I feel fear in the pit of my stomach', or 'my heart is broken', or something like that.

I'm trying to get across the picture that this is one unbroken process. In a sense 'I' am not doing anything – it's going on by itself. But the tacit assumption of thought is that 'I' am doing everything and thought is just telling me the way things are.

Q: No, the thought is 'the pain is being done *to* me'. You say something, and therefore I am hurt. And I actually feel physically hurt.

Bohm: But this thought is double. The thought is that the thinking is being done by *me*, and the pain is being done to me by *you*.

Q: You're saying that the pain is being done by me?

Bohm: By the same thought that does it all in the first place.

Q: Is it so fast because the emotion mediates the process?

Bohm: Emotion is very fast, that's true. The emotional centre is hit very quickly. But then there is another centre down in the solar plexus that takes longer; it may take two or three seconds.

There is an instrument called a polygraph. An electrode is attached to your finger and measures your skin resistance. When your autonomic nervous system is working, the machine deflects. If somebody says something disturbing to you, the needle deflects about three seconds later. It takes a few seconds for the impulse to get down the spinal column; it's in the pipeline for a few seconds, and then it operates. But since you don't see it going down the pipeline, you say that it worked independently – that it was a gut feeling, very important, or straight from the heart. Now, there may be gut feelings, or feelings straight from the heart, but memory can produce something very similar. That's where the difficulty is.

It is getting late. During the night you may want to go over this and think or feel it. We could start tomorrow by discussing whatever you may learn.

41

SATURDAY MORNING

Bohm: We discussed a number of points yesterday. We talked about the depressing state of the world, and the many problems confronting the individual and the society. We considered the notion that the source of all these problems is thought – that they are symptoms of something deeper, which is the whole process. We were saying that thought is not merely the intellectual activity; rather it is one connected process which includes feeling and the body, and so on. Also, it passes between people – it's all one process all over the world.

I suggested that we call that process a 'system' – a whole system in which every part is dependent on every other part. I also suggested that there is a kind of *systemic flaw* which is pervasive. So when we see something wrong with a part of this system, we bring another part to bear to try to correct it; but doing so will just add more, very similar troubles. We went on to say that it's not possible to solve our problems that way – rather, they may get worse instead of better – and that these troubles throughout the world have been going on for thousands of years.

Also, we said that when you try to look at what's going on inside you when all this is happening you may get unpleasant feelings such as pain or fear; and that instinct, as well as the whole culture, leads you to move away from looking at it. But it is necessary to stay with it somehow, in spite of the difficulty of doing so. That was what we were discussing at the end – that it is really worth doing because in this way we may learn something about how it all goes.

Now, I thought that people might have a few points to raise about what we've been talking about before we go on.

Q: During your conversation yesterday I assumed I was understanding what you were relating to us. But then there would be spaces of not understanding. When I went home I couldn't sleep. Finally I took a pad and pencil and wrote about ten or fifteen questions. After that I felt better, and fell asleep. Did my brain need that order and questioning, or whatever it came to?

Bohm: It's possible that the whole discussion leaves questions and the mind brings them up. If you're puzzled by something then it won't let you go. The major point is whether you are looking into what is going on and perceiving the incoherence – seeing what it means for yourself.

Q: What she just said might suggest that this is more of a psychosomatic process than we realize. We tend to think of it as a mental process, whereas maybe there's more involved that that. Maybe we have to keep an awareness for that other aspect of it.

Bohm: As I pointed out, we were saying yesterday that it is one system; the thoughts, the body, the emotions and also other people, are all part of one system. And when you raise questions intellectually they may affect the non-intellectual parts or vice versa – the other elements affect the intellect. Therefore you have to see it as one system. That's the crucial point, because otherwise you will never be able to deal with it. If it is one system you deal with all the parts.

Q: Is it possible to fit the concept of addiction into what you

were saying? I think of addiction as including not only physical addiction to things like drugs and alcohol but also various
kinds of thought addiction. There are supposedly positive
and negative ones. A negative thought addiction might be
racism. A positive one could be the whole legion of books
that have been written in the area of 'the power of positive
thinking'. Is this thought addiction part of the incoherence
you're speaking about, or can it be manipulated in positive
ways?

Bohm: If you engage in positive thinking to overcome negative thoughts, the negative thoughts are still there acting.
That's still incoherence. It's not enough just to engage in
positive thoughts when you have negative thoughts registered, because they keep on working and will cause trouble
somewhere else.

I'll just say a few words about addiction. One point is that
when you take a substance such as morphine, it acts by
covering up certain nerves or pain receptors so you don't feel
pain. Now, the body can create natural substances of similar
molecular structure, called 'endorphins', which do the same
– perhaps even better. In fact, people say that sometimes
soldiers who have been badly wounded in battle feel no pain.
They have a lot of endorphins at the time, and only later do
they feel pain. So that has a useful function in that it helps
them to survive.

But it is also possible for thoughts – reassuring thoughts
or pleasant thoughts – to produce endorphins. And then you
could in some sense become addicted to those thoughts,
saying 'I won't give them up; even if they're wrong I'll believe
them to be true'. You can't bear the idea that what you want
to think might not be true, because that would remove the
endorphins and then the pain would start coming back.

So you can say that there is a kind of addiction in the
thought process which is possible. In fact, it's one of the
things that holds us. The thought process is neurophysiological as well as intellectual and emotional. It has physical and

44

chemical elements. Medical investigators have demonstrated this when they do various scans of the brain. Every time you think, the blood distribution shifts all around and all sorts of changes occur inside; there are electrical brain waves that can be measured. Thus thought has, at the very least, a certain basis in this neurophysiological process; it can never be separated from it. That's something we have to keep in mind. And that process is part of the system we're talking about. Also, if you physically alter that process – by putting drugs into your body, for example – you've altered the system.

Q: Is there a space where a new thought comes in that's not conditioned, which enables us to have a dialogue?

Bohm: We will discuss dialogue later. For now I'll say that there may be a space, but we can start the dialogue without considering that question and then discover whether there is that space.

One point I wanted to emphasize last night was that we don't want to regard this system as an absolutely fixed monolithic thing which you can never break into. It's actually not all that solid. It has chinks and lets some things through, therefore there is an opportunity to do something. You can't control it, but opportunities do come up.

Q: What are the effects of the process of 'positive thinking' on our health? Wouldn't there be a schizophrenic duality between the fact of our negative thoughts and the illusion of the positive thinking?

Bohm: If somebody wants to engage in positive thinking it's only because he is already caught up in negative thinking. He wants to overcome that with positive thinking. But the best he can hope for is to fill his mind with positive thoughts so that the negative thoughts go into abeyance and don't bother him so much.

45

Q: The thoughts go to the basement and stay there.

Bohm: Yes, they're there; they are waiting. And when the person somehow feels weak or frightened or something happens, out they come; he hasn't actually dealt with those negative thoughts which are registered in his memory. People only say things like 'cheer up' to somebody who's already depressed. If he's depressed for some trivial reason that may be all right, but if he has some less trivial reason it won't go away. He may cheer up for a while, but the depression will come back. At the very best it's not a real solution, and at the worst it could bring in various endorphins and make him addicted to false thoughts, and so on. It is not a solution. We have to get deeper than that.

Q: Are you saying that we have a psychology in which our well-being is based on having affirming images, and that that psychology could never stand up as a real base for well-being because sooner or later we're going to get negative images?

Bohm: Yes, so long as we take these images seriously. If we can be cheered up by positive images we can be depressed by negative ones. As long as we accept images as realities we are in that trap, because you can't control the images. You may be getting some nice positive images from the people around you and then along comes somebody who gives you an extremely negative image. Then the very channels which made you feel good because of the positive image enable you to feel bad because of the negative image.

Q: It seems you're implying that in order to be really attentive to what's going on with thought, people would have to do so in depth. The psychological world would be the shadow side of the personality or the angry dogs in the basement –

what in psychology is called 'guilt'. It is always buried underneath and we're seeing it in other people.

Bohm: We have to let anything come up which is going to come up. But the point is that we have a mechanism for preventing it from coming up. The brain is already conditioned to keep it down. We have to understand that process.

Q: And that's culturally reinforced.

Bohm: Yes, it's always being reinforced. Let's say that things which are relevant would otherwise come up in consciousness, but there is a whole mechanism to keep them down.

Q: A kind of suppression happens even in some areas that are considered good. Some people won't accept anything nice being said to them because they don't see themselves as being good.

Bohm: It's all the same whether you say that you're wonderful or that you're guilty. It's just one image instead of the other. The fundamental process is not different whether you say 'I'm the greatest and the best', or you say 'I'm the worst, I'm guilty of everything'. It is the same process and the difference is rather secondary. If you say you are the best, somebody is going to come along to question that. And people often, for all sorts of complicated reasons in their past, find it easier to accept guilt.

Q: Is it worth questioning the process of either? Don't we have to get underneath that whole process and see that any image we have is not based on reality? So it's not a question of whether I should believe in the negative or the positive; it's understanding the whole thing in one piece.

Bohm: That's right. It is one system – the positive and the negative. The positive and the negative are two sides of the system. Anything positive is implicitly negative, and vice versa. Let's try to look at that.

Somewhere in the middle of the brain there are pleasure–pain centres. Researchers have access to those centres in animals. I once saw an article which showed a picture of a cat looking very pleased when they touched a pleasure centre either electrically or chemically. Then when they touched it a little stronger the cat looked very frightened. When they touched it a little stronger still, it looked enraged but somewhat pleased at the same time. Rage was pleasure.

What they said was that every time you stir up pleasure, all the pain centres around also come in to compensate. Every time you stir up pain the pleasure centres come in. There is always a mixture of the two. It's a very complex feeling. Suppose you stub your toe: you feel pain, but meanwhile the pleasure centres are set to work to overcome that. And when the pain goes away you then feel pleasure – it's left over. In other words, the pain has died away and the pain centres are quiet for a moment. But the pleasure centres take a bit longer to quiet because they were stirred up a little later, so one turns into the other. Likewise, the sense of fear and the sense of security will turn into each other.

Then the process gets more complex because we introduce words about it, saying 'this is pleasure, that is pain'. We've introduced this way of saying that things are either pleasurable or painful. If something is not pleasurable, the implication is that it might be painful. Or if you are losing the pleasure you had before, then there is an implied loss – there is pain. On the other hand, if you think that the pain is over then you are pleased by that. So pleasure directly implies pain, and pain implies pleasure. You can't separate the two – either at the level of chemistry or at the level of the intellect, or anywhere else.

The attempt to have constant pleasure must fail, because the pleasure centres get worn out. And the pain centres, having been stimulated to balance them, will then start to come in strongly. Thus there is no way to get pleasure constantly. If you were to try to do it I think you would discover that it would become painful. Pleasure is always a transitory phenomenon.

The pleasure–pain reaction is generally appropriate for the animal, but you can see that for thought it is not. The criterion for coherent thought is that it is true and correct. But if you can get pleasure or pain from thought then coherent thought is no longer functioning. Rather, the criterion has become whether the thought gives pleasure or pain, consequently that thought becomes destructive. If thought can be determined by pleasure or pain, that's already the beginning of a lot of trouble. And we get conditioned by that. We'll come back to all this a bit later.

Q: The endorphin feeling seems to be the best that we can do without transforming into another state of being. We seem to prefer to be in that, and spend our lives looking for ways to be able to keep the endorphins active.

Bohm: Anything that would give endorphins would be equivalent to taking morphine, or even better. You'd feel good for the time being. But you can't maintain the endorphins forever; it's bound to change. There are, for example, other chemicals which can cause anxiety, and there are still others that cause other reactions. They all go on to the receptors in a way you can't control. Therefore that process of pursuing constant pleasure is not really going to work. If you look at it you will find that the attempt to control the endorphins is not coherent.

Q: I find that out; still, the other state beyond doesn't seem to arrive.

Bohm: The 'other state' is projected by this system. If we start by assuming that there is another state then we have already gone into the system, because the projected image of another state is also producing endorphins. We have to see that the only right way to do it would be to say that we want to see what *is* – what is correct, what is true, what is coherent.

Q: That's not the same as seeking pleasure?

Bohm: No. But even if you do get pleasure from it, fine, except that your seeing may get distorted. I'm saying the key point is that this process is not coherent; none of it has any meaning – whether you have pleasure or pain or fear or whatever. When the process has sustained incoherence then it all has no meaning. Somebody may get great pleasure by deluding himself, an extreme case being 'I'm God' or 'I'm Napoleon'. And if he deludes himself sufficiently, perhaps he could keep out all evidence to the contrary. But you can't maintain this forever without destructive consequences.

So the attempt to live by pleasure or endorphins is not coherent. We are caught up in a process, in a system which isn't making sense. That's the first thing to notice. Then what do we do? I think we have to understand this process better.

Q: Does being aware of the system already bypass the chemistry, and therefore the thought is not getting hooked up into the chemistry of the endorphins?

Bohm: To some extent. But probably you would find it would get hooked up later anyway, because something would happen that comes in too fast or too powerfully.

Q: I didn't mean forever; but at the moment when you are watching this process unfolding, maybe you've, in a way, gone out the back door – away from the fear of the pain and the need for the endorphins.

Bohm: Let's say you may have begun to move on another level; or there may be another level that is awakening, which is not controlled by the system. That's a possibility.

Q: Aren't we starting this enquiry with the notion that 'I' am inquiring, 'I' have 'my' endorphins, and so forth? Right there might be a tremendous assumption.

Bohm: Yes, but we have to say all that. I am all the content of the system, but at the same time I may have a potential for more. That's all we can say. We're not assuming. We are exploring – do we have the potential for more than the content of the system?

Q: 'What' inquires might have nothing to do with endorphins.

Bohm: There may be a potential beyond the system. If it's true inquiry, then perhaps it is beyond the system. But don't assume it, because then it will be part of the system. Every assumption goes into the system.

There's another way we can look at this which gives some insight: that is to look at thought as a *set of reflexes*. Now, what is a reflex? 'Reflex' means 'to bend back', 'to turn back' – the same as 'reflect'. If you hit your bone at the knee, the knee will jerk. What happens is that the nerves carrying the signal meet somewhere; they cross over, perhaps in the spine, and go out as a signal to make your knee jerk. That's one of the most elementary reflexes.

We have a lot of reflexes, and they can be conditioned. For instance, dogs have a reflex that makes them salivate when they see food. A reflex means that when a certain thing happens, as a result something else happens automatically. Pavlov did an experiment where he rang a bell while showing food to a dog. He did this many times, and after a while the dog would salivate without seeing food, just from hearing the bell. Perhaps the bell reminded the dog of the food, or perhaps eventually it skipped that stage and the bell just made the dog salivate directly. But the reflex was conditioned by the bell; in other words, it was subject to another condition.

That is the basic form of conditioning – to repeat something quite often. It somehow leaves a mark in the system, in the nerves, and then a reflex has been altered. You can see the conditioning of reflexes all the time. In fact, a great deal of our routine learning consists in establishing conditioned reflexes. As an example, when you learn to drive a car, you are trying to condition your reflexes so that they will be appropriate. It's the same when you learn to write – you don't want to have to think all the time of how you're going to form the letters – or when you learn to walk or to do various other things. So certain reflexes are established and conditioned.

We've said that when we have a thought it registers in the memory. It registers in the form of a reflex. Memories often take that form – you see something and it reminds you of something or it makes you do something or it makes you see something in a certain way. Those are a kind of reflex. And conditioned reflexes can affect the feelings. Somebody may say something to you, and you get a certain feeling in response to what was said. It may frighten you, which could affect your adrenalin, and that could affect your thoughts; then one thought leads to another and that leads to another. You get a chain of thought.

You could say that elementary thoughts may take the form of a series of reflexes – such as, if somebody asks you your name you have an immediate answer. It's a reflex. With a more difficult question there's a way the mind searches in the memory for answers; there is a 'searching reflex' set up – the mind searches the memory, finds an answer that may seem to fit, and then that answer comes out and you can see whether it does fit or not.

I'm proposing that this whole system works by a set of reflexes – that thought is a very subtle set of reflexes which is potentially unlimited; you can add more and more and you can modify your reflexes. Suppose like a logician you say: 'All swans are white. This bird is a swan therefore this bird is white.' But then you modify this by saying 'I've seen that some swans may not be white.' And so on. Even the whole logical process, once it's committed to memory, becomes a set of reflexes. You think logically by a set of reflexes. There may be a perception of reason beyond the reflexes, but anything perceived becomes sooner or later a set of reflexes. And that's what I want to call 'thought' – which includes the emotion, the bodily state, the physical reaction and everything else.

I say that it's useful to look at this as a system of reflexes. A reflex just operates, as we've seen in the case of the knee-jerk. However, we don't usually think that thought is like the knee-jerk reflex. We think *we* are controlling thought and producing thought. That way of thinking is part of our whole background. But I'm suggesting that it's not generally so – that a vast part of our thought just comes out from the reflex system. You only find out what the thought is after it comes out. Now, this really overturns a great deal of the way we look at the mind or the personality or our entire cultural background.

So it's worth pondering that this whole system, which we are calling 'thought', works as a system of reflexes. The question is: can you become aware of the reflex character of thought – that it is a reflex, that it is a whole system of reflexes which is constantly capable of being modified, added to, changed? And we could say that as long as the reflexes are free to change then there must be some kind of intelligence or perception, something a bit beyond the reflex, which would be able to see whether it's coherent or not. But when it gets conditioned too strongly it may resist that perception; it may not allow it. Is that clear what I mean?

The point is that these reflexes serve us if they are not too rigid. And if they don't work, if they are incoherent, we can drop them or they may drop themselves. On the other hand, when the reflex gets very strong and rigid it won't be dropped.

I think there is a neurophysiological chemical reason for that. Every thought involves some change in the chemistry of the system. A strong thought with a lot of emotion, for instance, involves a bigger change. Or a constant repetition builds up the change. And both together make a very powerful effect. It's been observed that the nerves in the brain don't quite touch each other, but there are synapses which connect them. Researchers say that experience, perception, thought, and so on, establish synapse connections. We may assume that the more you repeat a pattern, the stronger those connections become; and after a while they get very strong, very hard to shake. You could say that something happens in the chemistry, in the physics, in the neurophysiological process. So this is not purely an intellectual problem or an emotional problem or even a physical problem. Rather, the reflexes get conditioned very strongly, and they are very hard to change.

And they also interfere. A reflex may connect to the endorphins and produce an impulse to hold that whole pattern further. In other words, it produces a *defensive* reflex. Not merely is it stuck because it's chemically so well built up, but also there is a defensive reflex which defends against evidence which might weaken it. Thus it all happens, one reflex after another after another. It's just a vast system of reflexes. And they form a 'structure' as they get more rigid.

Q: Isn't this the evolution of learning? Isn't this also how our bodies have evolved?

Bohm: It may be. But now the question is: are those reflexes coherent? According to the theory of evolution, incoherent systems don't last very long. This is called 'natural selection'. In thought, however, we seem to be able to keep up these incoherent systems of reflexes, at least quite a while. Sometimes the people who have them might not live very long, but in our society we have arranged conditions where we can go on with a lot of incoherence without actually leading to a selection process. The point is that reflexes can become incoherent and get stuck because of all these mechanisms.

Q: If you had to use another word for incoherence, what would it be?

Bohm: 'Inconsistency', 'Conflict'. What is incoherent may show up as contradiction, as stress.

Q: Inappropriate?

Bohm: Inappropriate, yes, if it's sustained. What I mean is that if there is sustained incoherence, it just keeps on going in spite of the fact that there is evidence which would show that it's incoherent. Now, we could say that an intelligent response on seeing incoherence would be to stop it, to suspend it and begin to look out for the reason for the incoherence and then to change it. But I say there is a defensive incoherence. An incoherent train of thought which gets attached to the endorphins will typically defend itself, because you will feel very uncomfortable when it is questioned; the questioning starts to remove the endorphins.

Q: Is there an analogy between incoherence and cancer?

Bohm: Cancer is an incoherent growth. It's incoherent with the whole system of the body, and it grows on its own. For some reason the cancer is not accepting whatever system the body uses to keep itself in order; it defends itself against it, and in fact even mobilizes the body to support it. I've read that certain kinds of cancers can send out chemicals to the body which cause the body to grow blood vessels to feed the cancer, which is a highly incoherent process from the point of view of the body.

Q: From that standpoint, any form of disease would be the same thing.

Bohm: Yes, a kind of incoherence. It's incoherent with the organism as a whole.

Q: Could we say that stress would be a crystallization of the system?

Bohm: Stress would be a lot of conflict resulting from this incoherence. You can see that it affects the chemistry, not only in the brain but all over the body, and produces further changes which keep on accumulating.

Q: Can we use the word 'reaction' with reflexes? Are these reflexes all physiological or is the reaction psychological?

Bohm: I want to emphasize that it is not just psychological. Every reaction is also neurophysiological. That's why I prefer to call it a reflex. Every reaction of thought is always simultaneously emotional, neurophysiological, chemical and everything else. It is all one system. In some cases that may not be important, but there is always a slight effect at the very least. And when there's a powerful conditioning then the effect is very great. I mean, when you just have a thought such as 'the cup is on the table' it's a rather minor effect; but some physical effect is going on just to say that.

Q: Could we say that anything we do or think that is out of harmony with the whole would be incoherence?

Bohm: It depends on what we mean by 'the whole'. It's hard to give a positive definition, but the basic sign of incoherence is that you're getting some result which you don't intend and don't want. And the other signs are contradiction, conflict, stress, all those things.

Q: Confusion?

Bohm: Confusion, yes.

Q: And also our action to try to get out of the confusion would be incoherent?

Bohm: We may have an inappropriate action. Within the system, the action to get out is part of the trouble.

Q: A moment ago it was asked whether anything out of harmony with the whole would be incoherence. But it seems we couldn't know what the whole actually is, and incoherence could only be in less than the whole.

Bohm: Some part is not coherent with the rest, yes.

Q: We've established limits within the whole. Perhaps our craziness as human beings might really be part of a greater coherence, by eliminating the species because it's such a reprehensible one.

Bohm: If you take a great enough whole then it's coherent. That is, the universe as a whole is coherent, and anything incoherent we do is just part of the coherence of the universe when we look at it that way, even though if we do something crazy we will get a result we don't want.

Q: So out of our level of incoherence we might try to become coherent, and that might be part of the incoherence?

Bohm: You could say that in the universe as a whole there's no reason to say there is incoherence. But we, in our particular structure, are not coherent. And a species that is not coherent either with itself or with its environment doesn't survive. That's part of the coherence of the universe. It is precisely because the universe is coherent that an incoherent species doesn't survive.

Q: Questioning our incoherence may also be part of our coherence. It could be the universal coherence that's stepping in and saying: 'Wait a minute. This isn't working.'

Bohm: It could be that that's part of it too. The question is then: which is going to prevail – this questioning or the old conditioning habits?

Q: Would you say that at the moment of conception, each human being is pretty much predestined to have this incoherence?

Bohm: I think it's built into the nature of thought that this is a possibility. And by now we have built up a society and a culture which implants it in everybody, even if it were not there. But because thought is reflex, the minute there were creatures who could think that much, there was the possibility that thought wouldn't behave coherently.

Now, I've outlined to you the possibility of conditioning the reflex – by repetition, by powerful emotions, by defensive methods, and other ways. And when it's strongly conditioned, the reflex could get stuck. Then there would come a time when that reflex was no longer appropriate but it wouldn't be able to change; therefore, that would produce incoherence. If something changes and the reflex doesn't, you have incoherence.

Q: What would you call death in relation to life?

Bohm: From the point of view of the species, death is part of this whole process. You could say that species have evolved in such a way that individual members last a certain time. Perhaps a certain kind of species would be better able to survive if the individuals didn't last too long. Other kinds could last longer.

Q: Doesn't it all end in death?

Bohm: It depends on what you mean by 'all'.

Q: Eventually – in the terms of time.

Bohm: But the universe doesn't end in death. This present universe may itself change, but perhaps there's something beyond that. So it's more accurate to say that any particular *thing* will end in death.

The question of death is very long and subtle, and we might get to it more, later. For the moment we can say that any material structure is always changing and cannot last forever. We need to ask whether our attitude toward death is coherent or not. There is no point asking whether death is coherent or not; death is just a fact. However, our attitude may not be coherent; maybe that's why death disturbs us so much.

Q: What are the criteria for coherence?

Bohm: There's no unique criterion for coherence, but you have to be sensitive to incoherence. And as we've said, the test for incoherence is whether you're getting the results you don't want.

Q: Then it's incoherent to have two things which are opposing each other?

Bohm: That's right. You can see that as contradiction and conflict and confusion. Coherence is sensed as harmony, order, beauty, goodness, truth, and all that everybody wants.

Q: Is the incoherence in the DNA, and are we born with that?

Bohm: Not this particular incoherence in thought. The possibility of our thinking is somehow in the DNA; as is the possibility that the thinking could go wrong, given a set of circumstances which will condition it to go wrong. And somehow in the history of the human race that has happened. We don't know whether it was inevitable. But considering the nature of our brain, we can see that it looks likely that this sort of thing could happen.

Q: Maybe that is why a Hitler is born.

Bohm: Well, it's also the society. It's the incoherence in the system as a whole which produced Hitler. It was not only his genes, but also he grew up in the Austrian society which had some very nasty incoherent features at the time. For instance, Hitler was beaten mercilessly by his father and he ran away when he was young. And he was beaten when he came back. Also, many people say that Hitler thought he had a Jewish ancestor, and this disturbed him because he hated the Jews so much. All of this must have muddled him up very badly.

So you can see there are all sorts of factors which added in. Maybe if they hadn't been there he would have been different. Who knows? That particular genetic structure born into that particular crazy society produced Hitler. Perhaps somewhere else it would have produced something else. Maybe in some other situation he would have been a great genius, because he did have some kind of ability.

Q: Would you say that any form of violence or disturbance would be incoherent?

Bohm: According to the dictionary 'violence' means 'the undue use of force'. And that's a kind of incoherence. If you're using force where force is not called for, that's incoherent. For example, if a problem arises in thought and you use force to try to solve it, that is uncalled for. Therefore, the attempt to deal with social problems by force is incoherent, because the problems all arise in thought. And violence will never solve the problem in thought.

Q: Do you think our cosmology is coherent?

Bohm: Probably not. No thought is fully coherent. The nature of thought is such that it is partial. We will discuss that later. But when we discover incoherence, our attitude can be either to move toward coherence or to defend the incoherence.

The kind of incoherence I'm talking about is the defence of the first kind of incoherence. Suppose you get used to certain reassurances of security and those reassurances give you endorphins. Then if evidence comes up that you're not so secure, you may reject that evidence. Not looking at the evidence *is* evidence of incoherence. As I've pointed out, there is a defence against seeing incoherence; and it is incoherent to defend against seeing incoherence. Now, that is the kind of incoherence I'm talking about, because you will never get rid of all incoherence in thought. Do you see what I mean?

Q: There's a defence against seeing incoherence because it interrupts the cosmology or belief system which we've all been imprinted with.

Bohm: It's much more complex than that. Our thoughts and beliefs have been connected to the endorphins, and when we question them we start removing a lot of endorphins from the brain. And suddenly the brain cells are jangling terribly, saying 'Quick, do something to stop this'. But the thing to do is to reject that.

Q: It seems, though, that we can't look at our cosmology.

Bohm: You can look at it. But that's only part of it; it's not the whole of it.

You cannot separate one part of the system from the other. If we had our brains working properly we could learn some cosmology and say: 'Yes, how interesting. A good chance to find a new cosmology.' But on the other hand, if we get a lot of comfort out of our cosmology, the brain cells will suddenly jangle and erupt when we try to question it; they won't give us a chance to look at it.

Q: Is envy a sign of incoherence?

Bohm: Envy is the same sort of thing. It's a comparison with somebody and saying that he has something I need or want. And then that makes you feel uncomfortable. Perhaps it removes a lot of endorphins from your brain cells. In any event, you get a very great discomfort and say 'the way to get back my sense of well being and comfortable feeling is to get what he has'. The potential for producing envy is an integral part of the brain, but it isn't necessary that envy be actualized all the time. If we can begin to see the process which is making envy, then the envy can come to an end.

Q: What about people who seem to glory and delight in misery? Is that producing some kind of endorphins also?

Bohm: They're probably getting some kind of pleasure out of it, although it's a very twisted kind of thought that gives pleasure from misery. But there are all sorts of ways to produce endorphins.

Q: Are you differentiating now between feeling bad and feeling good, saying they're not the same?

Bohm: No. I'm saying that you can feel either good or bad for twisted reasons.

Q: Is there a difference though?

Bohm: If the reasons are twisted then there's no difference. But if you feel genuinely good then that's different. Or you may feel bad because you're not physically well, and so on.

I think that the question of making good or bad feeling the key to your thought process is part of the incoherence. The question is: what about coherence in truth? Doesn't that take precedence?

Q: Then we're not saying coherence is good and incoherence is bad. We're just saying that is what they are according to their own thing?

Bohm: We're saying that there is a second order of incoherence which avoids facing the first order; this second order avoids facing evidence of incoherence. And also we're saying that that will produce all sorts of consequences which are destructive. Now, if you don't mind destructive consequences, OK go ahead.

Q: The only reason I bring this up is that we might get the notion in our thinking that incoherence is bad and it shouldn't happen, rather than that it's a conflict which appar-

THOUGHT AS A SYSTEM

ently wants to resolve itself. We're not in a position to say good or bad.

Bohm: Well, morals have no place at this stage. We're just trying to get a clear perception of all this. But you will discover that, in fact, you don't want to be constantly getting results which you don't want. At some stage you will discover that incoherence is producing all sorts of things you don't want, and perhaps you would like to get rid of it, or at least get rid of that second-order kind.

Q: A good clue would be to look at any form of violence, such as a person defending himself or wanting to change something that's frustrating. That would be a clue. That is incoherence right there.

Bohm: That's right. There are all sorts of clues. You have to become sensitive to those clues.

The principal thing to notice is that your incoherent actions are reflexes. You are not doing them on purpose. You don't know that you are doing them. It's the same as the way your knee jerks when you hit it, whether you like it or not. Similarly, when something touches those reflex conditionings, you just jerk. It produces the result which you don't want. So consciously you're trying to get 'A', but the reflex jerks and gives you 'B'. And you say: 'I don't want "B".' You don't know where it's coming from, so you fight 'B' while you keep on with the reflex that produces it. Do you see that that's where the problem is?

Q: Are we talking about the possibility of an interval? If you attack me negatively, I could hold my reaction in abeyance. Is that a way to deal with this process?

Bohm: You could try that. But I'm suggesting that we're

engaging in *learning* about this. We don't know yet what to do with it. We have to be interested in learning for its own sake, because if we have any other sake it's going to enter the conditioning.

You will find, nevertheless, that you do want to learn for the sake of making things better. But then you have to say 'well, that is also another reflex'. One reflex brings up another. So you say: 'I've understood now; and I've learned that doing things for the purpose of making things better may be a trap – it doesn't work in this area.' I've learned that, but I still do it because the reflexes still work. Then you need to say 'I have to learn about those reflexes which are diverting me'. What's characteristic of this is that I seem to understand that point but the reflexes continue. However, from what we said you will see that it's inevitable that that happens, because we first understand it on a certain abstract level – we haven't touched those reflexes. It's similar to the fact that you don't change the knee-jerk reflex just by saying 'I understand that my knee jerks whenever you hit it'.

How are we going to change the reflexes? That's the question. Understanding is important, but it will not be enough.

Q: Maybe something deeper happens after this intellectual understanding.

Bohm: It may, but very generally people find that it doesn't work. I'm saying we have to go deeper somehow; something more is needed. We'll come to the possibility later that somebody may get an understanding so deep that it does touch the reflexes, and then the thought process will change. But usually the understanding is a verbal understanding or an intellectual understanding or an image. That doesn't mean that it has no value, but it means that it is still too abstract.

Q: Maybe some 'homework' is needed for the understanding to go deeper.

Bohm: That's it, some 'homework' which will make it touch the reflexes. Unfortunately, we're often taught in school that when you have understood something abstractly you have understood it completely. But even there, when the time comes to put what you've learned into practice you often can't.

The thing we need to notice is that when we try this and it doesn't work, the first response may be: 'It doesn't work. I give up.' But in anything where you are serious you don't do that. If you're serious about something you say: 'Well, OK it didn't work. Why not?'

Q: I wonder if part of our difficulty is that we're imbued with the notion that we can understand, whereas the understanding you are referring to might have nothing to do with anything I know about or can grasp. Actual understanding might be something operating in an entirely different level and one would never say that one understood.

Bohm: There is some confusion about understanding; let's put it that way. We have to get further into the question of what it means.

People may see things they are doing wrong, but then when they're not paying attention they find themselves doing them anyway. And I think the reason for that is simple: this system consists of a set of reflexes, and that's exactly what reflexes do. For instance, if you brush your teeth in the morning you follow a routine. But you may very often start doing things as a routine when it is not the right occasion to do so. And if you pay attention you may find it's not working, and you say 'here's an incoherence'. You then stop.

So I think we need to pay *attention*. And if we think of thoughts as reflexes, it will help us to understand the system better and it will also begin to point to another level. The reflexes are on the level of the neurophysiology and the chemistry. The thought process is also chemistry; but it's a very much more subtle abstract level – the intellectual part of the thought process does not directly touch the reflexes.

Q: You can't think your knee not to jerk.

Bohm: Right.

Q: We are still on the sophist and intellectual level. Attention is really a potential to take us deeper.

Bohm: Yes, we have to get the kind of attention that will take us deeper.

But I do think that it's valuable to draw this 'intellectual map'. In any case the intellect has to be clear, because we already have a large number of *un*clear intellectual maps about this thought process. The whole culture has given us a lot of maps. For example, it's been said that thought and feeling and the chemistry are all different. That's a map which is misleading. There are a lot of maps of that kind which are wrong. What we need to do is to get somewhat free of those and to develop a more coherent map, although that alone is not going to do it.

Q: Isn't part of the problem the fact that the initial reflex is conditioned?

Bohm: Yes, but that's the nature of reflexes – to get conditioned when you repeat them. They will inevitably produce 'carry-on' effects.

Q: Suppose you intellectually understood this process, but that initial reflex was still so enticing that you can't drop it.

Bohm: That's the problem. You can intellectually understand it, but it still carries on. The enticement is part of the reflex, it's the chemical part of the reflex. The reflex produces endorphins or some other chemical, which will produce a sense of enticement.

Q: Then seeing deeper is a matter of perspective?

Bohm: I think that it's a bit more than that. Let's try to go into it as we go along.

We will have a break now.

Bohm: I'd like to extend this whole idea a little further. We inevitably have a kind of *thought about thought*, an intellectual map of the thought process which is sort of endemic; it's spread all through our culture – we pick it up here and there. For instance, saying 'think positively' is a kind of intellectual idea about thought, implying that you should control thought in order to deal with depression. There are all sorts of ideas circulating around.

I'm suggesting that we need to present some sort of map of thought which may be more coherent than the unspoken map implicit in our culture, because if we are being guided by incoherent ideas which are already part of our reflex system we will go wrong. And we can't just choose not to go wrong, because those incoherent ideas are already part of the reflex system. Therefore, the first step is at least to look at some other ideas which may be more coherent. Later we'll have to ask whether anything can really touch the reflexes, because if there is no way to affect them then we're stuck.

Now, I want to add something to this notion of reflex. One of the most powerful thoughts people have is the thought of *necessity*. It is much more than a thought. The word 'necessary' means 'it cannot be otherwise', and the Latin root means 'don't yield'. It suggests the emotional-physical stance of resisting, holding. That's the other side of the reflex system: when you say 'it cannot be otherwise', in effect you're saying:

'It has got to be this way. I have to keep it this way.' You have a hold. Something that is *necessary* is a very powerful force which you can't turn aside. Yet you may say 'I have to turn it aside'. Thus we establish an order of necessity, saying 'this turns aside for that, and this for that'.

This notion of necessity is crucial to our whole ordering of thought; as is its opposite, which is *contingency*. 'Contingency' means 'what can be otherwise'. If something can be otherwise, its meaningful to try to change it. If it cannot be otherwise, then there's no use trying. This will have a tremendous effect. If you think something is impossible to do, you are bringing in necessity by saying that it necessarily can't be done. Therefore, you can't do it and you will not try. So the assumption that something is impossible may well trap you into making it impossible. On the other hand, you may assume something is possible which is not, and just batter your head on a stone wall.

We have to get straight on what is necessity and what is contingency. And in each situation this is what you're doing all the time. You're trying to assess the necessity and contingency. We may see an object and say 'this will not turn aside from my hand'. I don't expect my hand to go through the object; if it went through I'd be very surprised. As an illustration, there was an exhibition of holography which projected a very realistic image of a ship, and two people came in who evidently didn't know anything about it. One woman came over and decided to take hold of the ship and her hand went through it. She didn't understand and there was a look of horror on her face. And she said to her companion 'let's get out of here'.

We count on the notion of necessity, saying: 'This will stand up. This will be stable. This cannot be turned aside.' We count on the earth being something that won't turn aside. And when it shakes we find it very disturbing – psychologically as well as physically.

The point is that the notion of necessity and contingency is always operating. Everybody is using it all the time without even thinking about doing so; it becomes part of our reflexes.

69

And this is important, because this also is connected with our idea of reality – things which are real won't be turned aside. They will sort of resist; they're pushing, and so on. Now, there are various ways of testing for reality. Things we consider real are stable, they resist, they have a kind of internal necessity that holds. The whole idea of reality is bound together with the concept of necessity, as in the example I just gave: if your hand goes through the ship it's a sign that it is not real.

The notion of reality is also clearly very important in our whole psychic make-up. The difference between being real or unreal or illusory is crucial. So the notion of necessity creates a powerful reflex – 'it really has to be that way'. If we not only add *emotion* and *repetition* to the reflex, but also add the notion of *necessity*, the reflex becomes very powerful – especially if we say 'it's *always* necessary'. Something may be necessary some of the time, but then it may have to turn aside at another time. But if we say 'it's always necessary', that means it is absolutely necessary, it cannot turn aside. For instance, if we say that the nation is sovereign, then that becomes absolute necessity and there's no way of turning that aside. And if two nations assert their sovereignty in the same place, what can they do? There is no way to turn aside, and therefore they have to fight. Or two religions in the same way – 'God is absolute necessity', and 'God has got to be this way and not that way'.

There are similar questions all through life. Wherever people are finding it hard to get along you will discover that they have different assumptions as to what is necessary or absolutely necessary. If you look at it you can see that that's what they're fighting about. One feels this is necessary and the other that, and they cannot turn aside. Negotiation is an attempt to make people turn aside for each other and to adjust and adapt, which admits that there is some contingency in what they thought was necessary.

The question of dialogue, which we're going to get into, is involved very much in what you assume to be necessary. The assumptions of what is necessary are what prevent dialogue.

They create a set of reflexes to defend with absolute force. They give power to the reflex.

The instinct of self-preservation is generally regarded as a very powerful set of reflexes built in by a set of genes, but the notion of absolute necessity will override that every time. You may say 'my instinct is to preserve life'. But if the country says 'it's absolutely necessary to risk it', then you have to risk it. Most people will feel that way. Or if you say 'God demands it', then the demands of God may override all the instincts. Or whatever it is. Your ambition may override the instincts, if it's absolutely necessary to achieve your ambition.

There's a tremendous force in this. This notion of necessity is not merely intellectual. It involves everything. It involves the chemistry, which means that all the adrenalin you need will be released when you have to defend your assumptions of necessity. Whatever is needed will be made available. And then too, this may have a very valuable side to it. If you are ever going to accomplish anything, you need some of that sense of necessity. If you don't think something is very necessary you won't have much energy to do it. You could say that nobody ever went through difficulties to accomplish anything without feeling that it was necessary. So if you feel that going into thought is necessary then perhaps it will continue against the difficulty. On the other hand, you may feel that some crazy incoherent thing is absolutely necessary and go on with that.

Therefore, it's important to pay attention to these notions of necessity – what is assumed to be necessary and absolutely so, and how it moves you. You begin to notice that. You get that feeling of urge. You're *impelled*; you have an impulse to act. 'Impelled' means 'being pushed from within'. Sometimes you are being *com*pelled, which is a bit stronger – a compulsive urge. Or *pro*pelled. Or perhaps even *re*pelled. But it's all the same process – it's necessity at work, giving a push.

Thus you feel an impulse and you say 'that's *me*, having an impulse'. You don't see that there is a system involving the thought beneath the impulse. And your *intentions* may arise in that system. Thus researchers have made electrical measurements and shown that there is some electrochemical process in the brain that precedes your conscious intention. The impulse is coming from the whole system. It's built up.

Now, it's important to see that this is all connected, because this is not a place where it's correct to break up things and to separate them. In some cases it is correct to separate things – such as saying that the table is separate from the chair because one can move independently of the other. But when things are tightly connected then we shouldn't separate them in our minds. We may *distinguish* certain things for the sake of convenience. The word 'distinguish' means 'to mark apart'. A distinction is merely a mark which is made for convenience; it doesn't mean that the thing is broken. It's like a dotted line, whereas when we represent something as divided it's a solid line. So in our minds we should draw dotted lines between thinking and feeling and chemistry and so on, not solid lines. Likewise, it would be good to draw only a dotted line between countries as well – because actually it's a distinction, rather than a division of two different things which are independent.

We have to be able to think of this clearly; even though, as I said, that by itself won't really change the reflexes. But if we don't think of it clearly then all our attempts to get into this will go wrong. Clear thinking implies that we are in some way awakened a little bit. Perhaps there is something beyond the reflex which is at work – in other words, something unconditioned.

The question is really: is there the unconditioned? If everything is conditioned, then there's no way out. But the very fact that we are sometimes able to see new things would suggest that there *is* the unconditioned. Maybe the deeper material structure of the brain is unconditioned, or maybe beyond. We'll discuss that later. It doesn't matter at this stage where it is, as long as it could act. If there is the unconditioned, which could be the movement of intelligence, then there is some possibility of getting into this.

We are saying that, perhaps unbeknownst to us, the unconditioned may have operated a little. We're not trying to say that the conditioning is absolutely solid and frozen, all and forever; that's the point. And if we are going to do this sort of thing that we're doing, to be coherent we at least have to suppose that there may be the unconditioned. If we don't suppose that, it may be then that we are totally incoherent in our very attempt to do it. If we say that there cannot be the unconditioned, then it would be foolish for us to try to do anything with the conditioning. Is that clear?

Q: If we made such a statement, we would have assumed a tremendous position of knowing.

Bohm: If we once assume that there cannot be the unconditioned, then we're stuck. On the other hand, if we assume that there is the unconditioned, again we are going to be stuck – we will produce an image of the unconditioned in the system of conditioning, and mistake the image for the unconditioned. Therefore, let's say that there may be the unconditioned. We leave room for that. We have to leave room in our thought for possibilities.

Q: Wouldn't we have to say more, in the sense that thought could never know that there is only the conditioned? It would be way past its bounds for thought to make such a statement.

Bohm: Yes, it's incoherent for thought to make that statement. It's fairly evident that thought doesn't know that much. If thought merely sticks to what it knows, it has no way of saying there is no unconditioned, nor can it safely say there is the unconditioned. Now that means what? That we don't know. But we may say we suspect that there is the unconditioned – we have seen evidence that there may be. We can go into this more, later.

73

Q: Is evidence of the unconditioned sometimes seen in creativity?

Bohm: Yes, some evidence. You could say the fact of creativity suggests that there is the unconditioned. But it doesn't prove it, because some people in artificial intelligence would say that what you consider creativity is merely a much deeper form of conditioning which you don't see.

Q: Even that would be better than the conditioning we have now.

Q: But that would just amount to expanding our limitations.

Bohm: We might still get incoherence. And incoherence with creativity has become more dangerous than without it. Without having created all these modern scientific things, we might be much safer. Thus, if we were still at the Stone Age level we could go on with our incoherence. We would be quite safe with our incoherence; we wouldn't have the means of doing very much. We could probably survive indefinitely. Actually, the evidence is that the Stone Age people were more coherent than we are anyway. At least their attitude to nature was more coherent. But even if they were as incoherent as we are they could probably survive, because they could not do that much damage.

But our creative technology challenges us. We have to be coherent. At least we have to move towards coherence, or else all sorts of disasters may occur.

Q: Can I work on my conditioning intellectually by realizing, for instance, that I don't feel good when somebody yells at me? Can I look at that without having expectations of the end result, of what it would be like if I didn't have this conditioning, and just let it be?

Bohm: But what happens then? Suppose you say 'I don't feel good when somebody yells at me'. Then you ask 'why not?'. What's the answer?

Q: I have to look within to see if there's any connection of similar groups of memories, that it's not really that particular person who's yelling but any person who's yelling.

Bohm: You have a general assumption there, don't you? That you are the sort of person who should not be yelled at, that it's absolutely necessary that nobody should yell at you. That seems to be the assumption. I think it's worth fishing around to try to put the assumption into words. It's important to get it into words, because otherwise you miss it – the brain is set up to hide the assumption.

Q: My understanding is that they have a right to yell.

Bohm: But not at you.

Q: No, that doesn't matter. What matters is why I am reacting to it.

Bohm: Let's say that before you got that far the first thing you found was that you were disturbed by somebody yelling at you. And now say why.

Q: Because it didn't make me feel good.

Bohm: But why is that? The feelings are bound up with the thoughts – we just said it's all one system. So maybe there is a thought that's behind it.

Q: The thought is 'I'm not good'.

75

Bohm: But why is that? If somebody yells, that doesn't prove you're not good.

Q: I believe that because of my conditioning.

Bohm: I'm saying that then you have another thought further back – which you may have forgotten from your parents – which says that whenever they thought you were no good they yelled at you. Accordingly you have an assumption in there, that 'whenever anybody yells at me it means that I'm no good'. And whenever I'm no good I feel uncomfortable. That's another reflex. Those two work together as a reflex: whenever anybody yells at me it means I'm no good, and whenever I'm no good it means I can't feel good. Now, those two thoughts are working in the chemistry.

Q: And I don't like what it does to me.

Bohm: You don't like that chemical effect; it's very disturbing. It makes sense that that chemical is disturbing. I mean, we can't criticize that.

Q: I'm asking if I can have a perception that can make the needle jump the groove in my memory into a space where that programming is cancelled.

Bohm: Well, that's what we're exploring: can it be done? But what's implied is that there has to be an electrochemical change in the brain. To reach an intellectual conclusion is not enough. We have a certain set of thoughts which have begun to point to the problem. And we have that same problem as before – that that alone is not enough to change the reflex.

Q: I realize now that it is the chemical part rather than the intellectual part that makes me feel uncomfortable.

Bohm: Yes, but it doesn't change. If somebody yells at you, you might still feel uncomfortable.

Q: But my experience has been that by realizing it, I'm letting the yelling come through. I'm feeling it in my body, not resisting it. And by not resisting it, it desensitizes the old misfiring of the synapses, or whatever, and it sort of reverses the process of what originally made me feel bad.

Bohm: It may. You can explore that. If you can stay with that, it may well do something like that.

Q: And suppose that happens, and I understand not only intellectually but also physically. Then a change is taking place. Do I then move to another conditioning?

Bohm: You may. There are a vast number of reflexes and we've only looked at that one. We have to get further, because one reflex gives rise to another and another. Behind these are all sorts of different reflexes ready to operate, and some of those may even bring back or recreate the reflex you think you've eliminated.

Suppose you say: 'OK, somebody yelled at me. And I can already begin to see the chemistry and all that, and I don't respond so much.' But you may have further assumptions which say: 'Whenever I'm too disturbed I can do nothing about it. I've just got to let it take hold of me.' Some people have that assumption; it's a common one. If the disturbance is extremely powerful then I have to let it take hold; that's necessity. So that assumption could also come in later – suddenly somebody who is very important to you really yells and it happens again beyond a certain intensity and the reflexes sort of take over again. That may happen; I don't say it will.

Q: When she has had that experience of the yelling activating

77

the chemistry, and if she has, together with that, a proper description of what is taking place, hasn't she then pointed in a new direction – even though someone else's yelling may cause her to react? She has been shifted.

Bohm: Yes, there's a shift in direction. It's a step, but still there may be more.

Q: However, people who have had that experience are never the same, even though they still react. They have a new opening, wouldn't you say?

Bohm: That opening can be lost if you don't keep it up. It requires sustained work.

Q: I don't think that means much has happened, only that the rigidity of the assumptions of the conditioning may be loosening a little bit and the person can feel more comfortable.

Bohm: A certain move has happened, but what I want to say is that we have to go very much further.

Q: Sometimes we can fool ourselves. We have, especially in this environment of people who are interested in these questions, the tendency to get very quickly into another assumption, saying: 'I've changed. Something happened in me and I'm transformed.'

Bohm: That would be an unjustified conclusion, without any evidence backing it up. That's the kind of thought that goes wrong – we jump to a conclusion, which gives pleasure or whatever. I'm saying you could just look at it; it's a step from which you could learn something.

Q: Provided the correct description accompanies it.

Bohm: You have to put it correctly in words, because the trouble is in the verbal sphere anyway – which has then affected the chemistry and all that. And in addition, all the other stuff is being carefully hidden by the reflexes; so if you don't get it into words it's not likely you are going to see it.

The problem is not just the feelings or the reflexes, and so on; it's the relation between all that and the words. The thought which was underlying the words was: 'Whenever anybody yells at me it means I'm bad.' Now, that is an assumption of necessity. 'Whenever' is *always*; it's something that is always so. That's why it's such a powerful concept. You often don't see the power of the assumption of necessity. So if you don't put it in words the reflex merely happens and you don't see the general assumptions back of it. But if you do put it in words you can see clearly: 'Whenever anybody yells at me it means I'm bad.' You need to put it in words and say 'that's the way I think'. And then you will get a feeling of that. But notice the assumption of necessity – that whenever anybody yells at me it's absolutely necessary to feel that I'm bad.

Q: It seems you can reflect on it in this way, and then you're changing the focus from 'they shouldn't yell at me' to 'what's going on in the mind that's making it so terrible or that's creating the reaction from my hidden assumptions?'. But is there some key to get behind the whole system of reflexes, rather than just examining each one and saying what the assumption behind each reflex is?

Bohm: We have to explore that. We examine it not in the spirit of trying to get rid of this or that reflex in particular, but rather in the spirit of learning more about the whole system, so maybe we learn something which can then be extended.

Q: It seems to me that the description needed wasn't simply 'I don't want people to yell at me and that bothers me'. Rather: 'Up to that point I believed that the disturbance in me was caused by someone "out there" saying something to me; and now I see that in response to words, *I* generate a disturbance in me.'

Bohm: But *I* didn't even do it. You could put it like this: 'I have a set of reflexes that did it, which came because I had concluded from a number of cases that it was absolutely necessary to feel bad whenever somebody yelled – that it was the right thing to do, that it was inevitable', and so on. That was the thought; and therefore whenever somebody yelled, the reflex simply worked – just like the knee-jerk.

Q: Then it isn't so much what we say; what is important is how we say it. Isn't that so?

Bohm: The yelling conveys a message.

Q: But in seeing that, haven't I in some sense shifted from thinking that the problem was external to me?

Bohm: You began to look at the real source of the problem, which is your own reflex. What you are pointing out is that I also had another reflex before; and whenever this happened, I added another reflex saying that this all has originated outside – that that's where the blame or the cause lies. So you see how the reflexes all work together. In order to prevent you from seeing the real cause of the thing, the reflex system has developed an explanation of why you feel bad – which is that somebody outside has done something to you. That's a rationalization.

Q: This seems to indicate that the problem was always within thought, not outside. Therefore it's just a projection.

Bohm: Yes. If your reflexes hadn't worked, nothing would have happened. If somebody says something bad to you in a language you don't understand, nothing happens.

Q: The tone of the voice sometimes may convey the meaning.

Bohm: Yes, yelling will work in any language. But somebody can say something to you very quietly which also means the same thing and you will feel bad, unless you don't understand what he says.

The point is then that you have to watch. It's crucial. Say, for instance, that you have a valid reason which makes it necessary for you to feel bad or to get angry or to be frightened or pleased, or whatever. Those feelings will affect the chemistry, and then the notion of necessity puts all the power behind it. You don't notice how often it's there implicitly rather than explicitly. Thus, it's very important to get it there explicitly so that you really see it is there, because the whole system is set up to prevent you from seeing it.

Freud used to talk about repression of unpleasant memories and traumatic memories. And you might ask: 'How could this be? You must first remember something in order to be able to repress it.' It seems to be paradox. But it's not a paradox, because our memory always has a vast content. A lot of it comes up which is irrelevant, and we have a lot or reflexes set up to try to select what is relevant, even in normal healthy memory. Now, those same reflexes can be set up to repress, to push down this unpleasant material. They simply respond to that material automatically, like the knee-jerk, and get it down; you don't need to do anything in particular. The whole system is set up to do that sort of thing, so it's really very hard just to look in there and see anything. But if you get a hint or a clue and can then put it in words, you can begin to see at least what the thought is. And you watch what the words do to your chemistry.

Q: Something happens to thought when we express it. It

makes it solid, it makes it real, we relate to it. If I don't express it, thought can take over my mind and I lose 'me'; but if I bring it out it becomes more real and then I can look at it.

Bohm: Yes, it's implicit when you don't put it in words, and it can do all sorts of things. But now make it explicit and then you can at least see that thought is doing it. So you're getting some perception. By bringing it out you can see that this is what is happening, whereas if you don't make it explicit you can't see that thought is involved at all. And therefore you say 'this is an emotional problem', or 'somebody out there has done it'. You give various explanations.

Q: As you put it into words, though, isn't it just as important to be aware or connected to the response in the body directly?

Bohm: That's what I mean; I'm saying to watch not only the words. When you say the words – the true words expressing the way you really think – your body is going to respond. You may say 'I've been hurt by that person; I'm very angry', and then you find out in words, 'I'm angry because he did this and this and this; and when anybody does this and this and this to me it's only right and necessary for me to get angry or hurt, or whatever'. Then if you have found the right words, and you watch, you will see that the body responds. That will be a nice demonstration of how the system works.

Q: Do you mean words like 'I've been hurt'?

Bohm: The words which express the real thought behind your hurt. Suppose you say: 'I trusted that person. He was my friend and I counted on him and then he said those terrible things about me. It's completely unjustified. It's traitorous behaviour. This was really something that was not

82

justified, not right. Worse – he betrayed me, he attacked me, he had no reason to do this.' You think of all those words and you will see the effect on the body. If you have found the right words, if you have found the words which express the way you are actually thinking, the body will be affected.

Q: At first we have an intellectual anger, and as we express it the body picks it up and we find out we're emotionally angry. And the next thing you know our voice is getting loud, or whatever.

Bohm: And then you find that you're physically angry; namely, you tense all over the body. And if you stay with it you find you will finally get the impression that this is nothing but a physical process. That's crucial, because you'll see this means that thought is part of the physical processes of the body, a very subtle part.

Q: It seems I can reflect on some disturbing emotion I've had and discover this underlying assumption of necessity. But often, even though I can say intellectually that it isn't really necessary, there's still a strong feeling that it is. I don't want to let go of it.

Bohm: That's the reflex. What I'm suggesting won't cure it. It is in the chemistry, it's not only in the intellect. This is being done to learn and not to change anything, because if you're trying to change anything it won't work. That is crucial to see.

So you find the words which do this and see how those feelings are affected and how the body is affected – just simply to learn. It may make a bad feeling go away; if so, fine. But it's not the purpose to make it go away.

Q: Then we're trying to get some perception into the process?

Bohm: Yes. In fact, if it goes away too easily you will miss seeing it and you won't have a chance to learn how it works.

Q: The purpose is learning, not changing.

Bohm: Not changing. Something may change you when you learn, but that's a by-product.

Q: Our conditioning tells us it's not nice to be angry, it's not acceptable to cry. And when we do fill up with emotion our conditioning tells us we're not supposed to feel that.

Bohm: That's the same thing. The conditioning is what we've been talking about. The conditioning is what makes us angry and the conditioning says 'you shouldn't be angry'. It's all the same. Then you may find that you have to put *that* in words, saying 'I believe it's absolutely necessary for me not to be angry', and begin to look at that. So those are more words. The point is that this is a system, and it sort of spreads out and out and out. Therefore, you don't expect to get it all right away by this procedure.

Q: We can't really ever expect anything, in the sense that any trying to move in there and take hold of something would be part of the system moving. And what you're suggesting lies outside of the system.

Bohm: Yes. I'm saying that we don't try to *do* anything. We're just learning – aware, attentive, learning.

Q: Is that implying that the way we are in the system is like being in some sort of a hypnotic trance?

Bohm: That's exactly what hypnosis is. Hypnosis is the use of the word to operate the system. You accept the word of the hypnotist as to what is necessary, and then that's all there is to it.

Q: When we are aware of the system as a whole – of the physiological process, the psychological process, the whole thing – the description seems to be accurate. It comes out of that awareness. But when the intellect wants to find the right word to describe the process, my experience has been that it doesn't work as well.

Bohm: I'm not suggesting you do that at this stage. I'm saying to find the word that makes the process go with full strength. It's like saying: 'I've got a piece of machinery. I want to make it go slowly so I can look at it – not spin with tremendous speed so I can't see it, nor just stand still so I don't see how it works.'

Q: Do we find what the button is?

Bohm: The button is the word.

Q: I still don't understand the button. Is it having just a very accurate description? Is that what you're saying?

Bohm: What we need is a *correct* description of the way you are actually thinking. Usually we don't put in words the way we really think. We won't admit to ourselves the real nature of our thoughts. If you are hurt you usually say 'he hurt me', or 'I'm hurt', or 'I'm not hurt'. You say all sorts of things. Those words will just lead you astray, because they will not be the thoughts which are actually working. They will just muddle it up.

Suppose we say: 'I don't know exactly the words, but I'm going to experiment and try to find them – the words which

85

express the thoughts that are really working, which are now only implicit. I want to make them explicit.' It may be that when I use those words, I feel worse. Therefore, my instinct is not to use them. But I say 'no, this is necessary, really necessary, truly necessary to get into this'.

Q: We dig until we find the words.

Bohm: Yes. So I say: 'It's truly necessary. I've seen why it is necessary. The fact that it hurts a little doesn't matter.' If you had a toothache you would go to the dentist and it could hurt; but you would say that it's necessary for him to drill or whatever, otherwise your tooth will decay. Likewise, you say: 'OK, I'm going to dig a bit. It may hurt, but it doesn't matter. I want to find out what is going on.'

Q: Can you give an example of what you mean by 'finding the words'?

Bohm: Suppose you are angry and say: 'I'm angry. He kept me waiting two hours. What did he mean by keeping me waiting so long? He takes me for granted. He doesn't consider my value at all. He does whatever he pleases. He probably had something better to do and he ignored me. He kept me waiting here and my time is valuable. He just doesn't consider me properly.' Depending on what it is, you find the words which express the real reason which seems to make it necessary to be angry – to justify it, make it right and necessary. 'Anybody would be angry in this case. Anybody treated this way would be angry. It's absolutely necessary and universal. I'm really right.' And so on.

Maybe we should stop now and resume this afternoon.

SATURDAY AFTERNOON

Bohm: At the end of the morning session we were discussing what we called a 'system', and saying that it seems valuable to try to learn something about this system. We said that the core of this system is really thought, though it involves all aspects of our being. We talked about the way the system works, and said that through observation you may be able to see this process happening and thereby learn something about it. Also, we were saying that with all sorts of emotional disturbances, such as anger, you could first find the words which will stir up the disturbance so that you can then get something to observe. In this way you can learn about the relationship between the word, the thought and all that follows – the feeling, the state of the body and so on. Of course, in doing that you are suspending the anger – holding it in front of you, so to speak. It's not so strong that you feel you absolutely must express it, nor are you keeping it hidden.

So you're beginning to get acquainted with the system, with how it really works. However, if you don't have that element of accurate language or an accurate representation in thought, then you don't see the system because the core of it is missing. Thought generally has it that *you* just 'see' what is happening; then the next thought comes along and says 'what is happening is something that is independent of thought'. And thus you get caught in that same fault again. The point is that you have to see this, to be actually seeing that this is happening – that thought is behind this system.

87

Otherwise the system seems to stand by itself, independent of thought.

Take any company, such as General Motors, as an example of something organized by thought. We have the thought that it exists and has a certain structure. But it is that very thought which ties the factories and everything else together as a company. What we consider to be General Motors is entirely organized by thinking. Except for that thought – I mean, unless people believed that it existed – it wouldn't exist. There might be the factories and buildings and all, but people wouldn't know what they're supposed to be doing or how they're supposed to be related, and so forth. The thought is at the core of it, and there is a whole system which develops out of that.

Now, we want to be able to see our system of reflexes in operation; and I'm suggesting that we have to have it there in front of us to see it, but suspend our reactions.

The second point about the use of language is that after you see something about how the system is working, you should also put that into words, because you want to inform the thought process of what you have seen. In other words, you may see something; but if the thought process doesn't know about it it will just go on as before. The thought process itself doesn't 'see'. It can only get information. Its typical way of getting information – on such an abstract level anyway – is from words. Therefore, I'm saying that it is essential to use words to elicit this thing, to make it visible to thought; and also we may then use words to state what we have seen. But we don't want to do it the other way around – to say 'this is the way it is', and then to see it that way. If it's done that way it leads to trouble, to illusion, which I'm going to discuss as we go along. This is a key point.

Are there any further questions before we go on?

Q: Are you saying that words will bring out memory, and that memory creates objects? By using the word, are we objectifying the memory?

Bohm: No. By using the word we are not only bringing out the memory, but we're producing the actual state which we are trying to explore – such as anger. We find the words which will bring up that previous anger that is still simmering. You've forgotten about it perhaps; however, it's still there on the reflexes, ready to spring again into action any time something of that nature happens. And if it does happen, it will happen so fast that you may not get a look at it. But if, instead of waiting for something to happen, you bring it up by using the right words, then you do have time to look at it. And one of the big things you will be able to look at is that the words are doing it. If the words were not there you would miss the main point. That means that *thought is doing it*. The words represent thought.

Q: If we think that we're not using words, are we still using words but just missing the fact that we're using them? Or are we thinking in some kind of other language?

Bohm: There may be another language. There may be an image language. There is an implicit thought which 'goes without saying'. It says implicitly 'whenever anything like this happens, I've got to react in this way'. That's the thought. It just reacts. And remember that the thought spreads out into all the other reflexes; therefore the thought is still going on in another form. For example, if I wrote it out on paper it would still be the thought but in another form. It can take many, many forms. It could be put on a television set. It could be carried by radio waves. It can be carried by all the reflexes. They're all part of that thought. They are different forms of that one thought. It's very important to see this – that this thought goes out and spreads all over the world. Other people pick it up and they make it part of their reflexes. But it's all thought.

The point is that the words are a way of bringing the thought into evidence, whereas often it works implicitly without your being aware of it. If you have a reflex that a certain kind of food disgusts you, you will get a sense of disgust when you see or smell it. But that disgust could have been programmed into you by some sort of words very early in childhood. That's still thought. That expression of disgust is basically thought. That's what controls it, that's what makes it happen. It's on the reflexes. So thought spreads all over the place in many, many different forms.

Q: We're just not aware of it.

Bohm: Part of the reason we're not aware of it is because of our culture, which tells us that thought is only intellectual and therefore it's no use looking after this other stuff. We might become aware of it if it weren't for that.

Q: By doing this, can we focus and see our real intention, not just what we are telling ourselves?

Bohm: We can see what is really happening, and see that this happening is producing part of our intention. If there is a valid necessary reason to be angry or to be impelled to do something, then you will get that intention out of the thought. If you say 'it's necessary for me to do my job', you find yourself getting the intention to do it. The intention can flow out of the thought, so the intention is still part of the thought.

Q: You said that we need to put what we've understood into words, and then communicate it to the thought process. How do we keep that from becoming another system?

Bohm: There is a danger that it will happen. We'll have to discuss later how this may happen and what could be done with this. But I'm saying it is necessary – that the thought process will not know what has been seen without some way of translating it into thought.

90

Q: Anyway, isn't one of the ideas to bring out the assumptions that are already in the thought structure? So it won't harm that much if they go back in, because they're already in there.

Bohm: Well, we're bringing out the assumption and we may then form a new reflex and make a habit of it. We could go wrong again. But I'm saying that we're just learning about it now; we're going into it, we're not actually trying to change it. That's the crucial point. If we once think we are trying to change it then we get into all the tangle of questions. But we're saying that whatever happens is grist for the mill. And if it happens that you form a new reflex, then you can learn about that.

Q: A lot of times I look at it the other way around – that we're not aware of the intentions out of which the thoughts come. It seems a little strange to me to put the emphasis on the thought.

Bohm: Many of our intentions are reflexive; they just come out automatically. They're coming from reflexes, whose basis is thought. The intention is *implicit* in the thought. You will be impelled to do something if something is 'necessary'. If somebody says 'you must do it, it's necessary to do it', or 'doing this will give you something you really want', then from that thought you will get the intention to do it.

We have the picture that there is 'somebody' inside us who is given all this information and then decides to have the intention to do something based on that. I'm suggesting, however, that that is not so.

Q: I'm thinking of cases where the person for some reason has to do something and then will generate thoughts that justify it.

91

Bohm: That's the next step. He may have one thought saying 'I must do this'. He has another thought saying 'it would be wrong to do it'. And he gets a third thought which justifies it anyway. The whole thing is one reflex after another. I think we have to see this system just working, working, working. Now, perhaps somehow intelligence can come in and get us out of this. But I'm saying that as long as the system works, you don't know what is happening any more than you know why your leg should jump when the knee bone is hit.

Q: Are you saying that the system is working by itself reflexively, mechanically, but it gives the impression that there's a 'me' as a centre?

Bohm: Yes. The system contains a reflex which produces the thought that it is *I* who am doing everything. It has a very elaborate system of covering up what is happening. We'll go into that, but it will take some time to do so; and I think we should go on from here if nobody has any urgent question.

I wanted to say more about thought. Thought is *incomplete*. The thought of the table doesn't cover all about the table. It picks up a few points about it. But clearly the table actually involves a vast number of things – its atomic constitution, all sorts of structure inside the material, how it's all related to everything, and so on. Our thought of it as a table is a simplification, or an 'abstraction'.

One way of looking at it is to say that thought provides a *representation* of what you're thinking about – the way an artist makes a picture which represents somebody but isn't somebody at all. Sometimes a few little lines are enough to represent that person, but clearly the person is far more than that; there is an immense amount which is not in the representation. Likewise, thought does not provide complete information or a complete picture or account of the thing it is supposed to be about. The thought of the table has only a few salient features, and also it's somewhat ambiguous; the thought of 'table' includes a lot of possible things that might be tables, such as all sorts of strange shapes and sizes. And then, occasionally, something comes along which you wouldn't expect to be used as a table. Thought is constantly adding different forms and shapes and such.

The example I've given is that the word 'table' calls up a representation in your mind of an image of some sort of typical table. There are countless forms an actual table could take. When you see an object which fits one of those forms or somewhere between those forms you may immediately recognize it; or if it is similar to those forms, even in some vague way, then it may still call up the notion of table, or the word 'table'. You can see that that's a kind of reflex. The various representations of 'table' are all put together. So when you look at a table there is a reflex in your mind. You don't actually utter the word 'table', but there's a potential reflex: 'that's a table'. If somebody were to ask you, you would immediately say 'that is a table'. The information is there in your mind, already on tap.

Therefore, a thing is recognized by the fact that it would fit a particular representation – it would be one of the possible forms of that representation. And any form of that will operate the reflex, and consequently you recognize it. Then when you think about it, you can think of all the things that are attributed to it and associated with it, and also connect up to other reflexes. Everything you think about is connected to reflexes which will involve what you can do with it. In the example of the table, the representation of the table in your mind is connected to reflexes involving what you can do to the table – that you can put things on it, or whatever. So you are already automatically ready to put something on there if the occasion arises.

Can you see how it's all connected up? The intellectual reflexes and the visual reflexes and the emotional and the physical and the chemical and everything are all connected up, so that you are ready immediately to take action. If it turns out that the object is not a table, it won't do what you expect. Then you say that it's incoherent. And if your mind

93

is working right you say: 'Something is wrong. I've got to change something.'

That's the way thought works. It gives you vast amounts of connected, logically interrelated information. Also, the symbol is somewhat open, it's ambiguous. The word 'table' is the symbol, whose meaning is ambiguous. It can include all sorts of other things. It has a tremendous potential for connecting things up.

You could say that the earliest thoughts before there was language would probably have involved images. Somebody raised that question: that before a child can use words, it probably uses vaguely defined images to stand in for the things it's thinking about. For instance, animals will see a part of an object and expect the whole, and so will very young children. It seems clear that part of the object can call up the whole, or objects that are vaguely similar could call up the whole class. It makes a reflex – that symbol makes a new reflex which connects all the other reflexes. Everyone of these objects that the symbol can stand in for has in itself a set of reflexes of what you can do with it, and that symbol connects it all. It's another reflex which connects all those reflexes.

So you begin to see thought organizing itself into a very complex, rich structure. I've hardly begun to touch on it; it includes thought, logic, reason, etc. You form very abstract symbols. For example, we talked today about the symbol of necessity and contingency – the two words. If you ask 'what are they?' you are unable to imagine what they are. I mean, you have no picture of what is necessity or what is contingency, but you have a vast number of things with which those words will connect. And any time you want to bring order into what you are seeing, one of the things you have to do is sort out what is necessary and what is contingent in that particular situation.

Another set of very abstract things is the *general* and the *particular*. The general is the reflex of inclusive and the particular narrows it down. And you treat things by the general and the particular. This table is something general, but the particular is also worked out; the table is made of wood, it is a certain shape, it's right here, and so forth. There are a vast number of things. And if you were to try to find out how all this thought process works, you could probably spend a lifetime and still not get there.

I say this to show that thought is not just the culprit, that thought is not pure wickedness. We have this whole very subtle and very complex structure – which we probably know very little about – that does everything for us. Thought is part of a system which includes all our reflexes, our relations to other people, all that we do, all our society, and everything. But it has a *flaw* in it.

As I said, thought works by representation – by a symbol and by a representation. A symbol stands in for the thing. A word is a symbol. You can use simplified images as symbols. The Chinese ideographic language came originally from pictures, and they were finally simplified and became mere symbols. But the alphabetic symbol is still more powerful, because it need have no resemblance whatsoever to what it represents. It's far more flexible. Such is the power of language.

You have innumerable symbols, and the symbol produces a representation; it presents the thing again, as it were. It gives you a kind of feeling for it. You can, for instance, represent a human face by a circle with two dots and a little triangle for the nose and then a mouth. If the mouth is curved up it represents a smiling, happy person; if the mouth is curved down it represents somebody who is unhappy and frowning. If you look at that, you will get the feeling of a smiling, happy person or a frowning person. It's a kind of representation of the meaning of the thing.

And representations can get more and more detailed, become more like artists' pictures. They may be diagrams, they may be blueprints, they may be all types of things. That's all thought taking different forms. Every one of those things is thought. You have to keep all that in mind.

Q: This level below the verbal, is it another system of symbols – pictures, perhaps?

95

Bohm: Pictures or lines. Very simplified pictures, or even blobs. Just enough there to stand in for something. And it would seem to me that a child who doesn't yet talk could probably do quite a bit of thinking through that. For example, the psychologist Piaget claims that a child who sees an object disappear behind something and then reappear acts as if he thought that the object had vanished and a new object had appeared. And at some stage he learns that it is the same object; but to do that he must have a symbol for that object, because he doesn't yet talk. He could have a vague picture of a blob – he doesn't have to have the exact picture of the object.

So there's a kind of preverbal symbol, and there may be others that we don't know about. Language is on top of all this. But when we learn to talk we forget this, and we don't recognize that these symbols are still part of our thought. They seem to be something else.

Q: Is this what you were speaking about earlier in terms of bringing these things up into the verbal and understanding them?

Bohm: At least getting a look at them.

Q: As you talk about this it seems that it's true, that there's this whole underlying level of pictures going on.

Bohm: And feelings as well. You see, Einstein didn't talk until he was fairly old. And he said that a lot of his thought consisted of feelings he couldn't describe, which may have taken the place of a certain amount of verbal thought. Therefore you might imagine that a little child sometimes represents things by feelings.

Q: When you start to bring these up and verbalize them it seems to elicit some level of clarity. They may be missed otherwise. But are we to be selective about this? It seems to be going on all the time. Can we constantly be bringing these up?

Bohm: No, we can't. We're just learning about it. We're not trying to *do* anything. It's crucial to see that we're not trying to achieve an objective; we don't have a programme or a goal that we could define. We are learning. I'm trying to say that here is something we didn't know about this process. It may be relevant, it may not. The fact that we know it may turn out to be helpful in some context. And we may be able to observe some of it by bringing it up. By bringing it into words we might get a connection to some of the other aspects of the process and get a better feeling for how it is working. One of the troubles is that this thought process is going on and we don't know at all how it's working. And when we don't know how it is working we very quickly regard it as something else: as non-thought.

Q: What we're doing is making a better map.

Bohm: Yes.

As I've pointed out, one of the key difficulties has always been that thought does something and then says that what it is doing is not thought. Thought creates a problem and then tries to do something about it while continuing to make the problem, because it doesn't know what it is doing. It's all a bunch of reflexes working.

Remember that 'thought' is a past particle. It's what has been registered in the memory. That registration is through a set of reflexes; so whenever a form appears which fits that whole set, that symbolic representation will stand in for whatever fits actually being perceived. For example, if it fits the representations that would be brought up by the word 'table' then you get all the reflexes to the table right away, which makes it very useful. But you can also make a mistake and make a wrong movement; then you are incoherent and you have to say: 'OK, it's wrong. I've got to go over it.'

I'm discussing how thought would properly work – and does in fact work in many areas – first, to show that thought is not all bad; and second, because to understand what has gone wrong we should have some understanding of how it would work when it is right.

Q: Is this the difference between thinking and thought as you described earlier?

Bohm: Thought just works automatically. But when you're thinking, you are ready to see when it doesn't work and you're ready to start changing it. 'Thinking' means that when the thing isn't working, something more is coming in – which is ready to look at the situation and change the thought if necessary.

Q: Is thinking an element that's outside of thought?

Bohm: It's a bit beyond thought. Let's put it that thinking is not purely the past; it's not purely a set of reflexes in the past.

Q: Would thinking be more 'of the moment', more energized, and thought more passive in the past?

Bohm: The past is *active*. That's the trouble. The past is not really the past – it's the effect of the past in the present. The past has left a trace in the present.

Q: Then the thinking would be even more energized?

Bohm: Yes. The thinking will be more energized because thinking is more directly in the present, because it includes the incoherence that thought is actually making. It may also include allowing new reflexes to form, new arrangements, new ideas. If the reflexes are all somewhat open and flexible and changeable, then it will work nicely.

Q: If I understand you clearly, you're saying that by looking at these primal feelings and thoughts and images, we have a certain opportunity to look at them again with more energy.

Bohm: Yes. We see them right there, and we are able to look at them with something which may be beyond the conditioning. Then the way we look would not be entirely conditioned, therefore we say it's more alive, or whatever. We're saying that we need to look in this way because it is very important to come into actual contact with this system which really rules our lives. It's very necessary – I've explained all the good things it can do, and how it works when it works properly, and so on.

Q: Can thought deceive us that it's thinking when it is not really thinking?

Bohm: It can deceive us about anything and everything. There is no limit to its power of deception. You could say that every trick we know, thought knows in the next moment. If we see a trick, then in the next moment thought has it there in the reflexes. In other words, thought is us – thought is not different from us.

Q: We are the deceivers and we are the deception.

Bohm: Yes, thought can do all that deception. But I've discussed how thought works when it is not deceiving. And it gets into this trouble which comes for many reasons. It's hard to analyse it. One reason is that ultimately the chemistry is too rigid, all these connections are too rigid. Or you could say that there is the thought of absolute necessity, which provides a hold on the whole thing. But they all work together.

Q: How is absolute necessity different?

Bohm: There could be a view of absolute necessity as just a perception, saying that at this moment you clearly have to do a particular action. But suppose you also say 'it's absolutely necessary for me to achieve my ambition, or to do various things'. That may be the past – it may be this whole system saying that.

So we have this situation: thought provides representations, which we can produce, outside or inside, as symbols that we can communicate, and which also hold everything together and connect everything.

Q: And the mass media?

Bohm: The mass media carry them all. They disseminate them. That's a good word – 'disseminate'. The symbols act like seeds. The media scatter them, and then those representations all become seeds of further reflexes. For the people who receive them they become new reflexes – they take root and become new reflexes. That's all a system.

And you can see that thought is inherently going to be incomplete. It can at best provide an abstract representation, it will not contain the thing itself. The thing itself is not only more than could be contained in the representation; but additionally, thought is not always right. The thing itself is always in some way different from what we think it is. It is never exactly what we think.

Also, some of our thought is mistaken when extended. For

100

example, people believed that Newton's laws would hold forever because they held for several hundred years. And yet quantum theory and relativity came in and overturned them. During the late nineteenth century, Lord Kelvin, one of the leading theoretical physicists, said that it was no use for young people to go into theoretical physics. He said that the major discoveries of physics were finished, and that what was left was only a matter of refinements and the next decimal points. However, the thing didn't work out that way. Nevertheless, some physicists now talk about a 'theory of everything'. They don't have it but they say that they're going to have it, they expect it.

Thought is always trying to claim that it knows everything. It has that tendency in it, and we have to say why. This is a very dangerous tendency, which leads to self-deception. It doesn't leave open the unknown. It doesn't leave open that the thought is only a representation. And you must leave room in your thought for something more and something different. Healthy thought requires that it intrinsically be built so that it always has room for that. I'm saying that whatever the representation is, it could be something more and something different. At most we could say that as far as we know a certain representation may be accurate. That leaves room for something more and something different. Now, that would be healthy thought, proper thought. Orderly thought would have to have that form and structure.

But a great deal of our thought doesn't have that. For example, religious thought often doesn't have it. A lot of our political thought doesn't have it. Even a lot of our scientific thought, as I've just explained, doesn't have it. That's a crucial point: one of the ways thought goes wrong is that it claims, implicitly at least, to be able to know everything – that it could get rid of uncertainty and get rid of the unknown. There is this drive in thought to say that it will eventually get hold of everything. I don't know whether that drive has always been there; but it is there, and as civilization develops it seems to get even stronger.

Such thought gives a sense of security. A lot of thought is

101

aimed at increasing our security. And in a legitimate way it does provide for greater security. We use thought to store up food, to acquire shelter, and do various other things. But then thought gradually begins to extend and say: 'I not only need that kind of security, I need other kinds. I need emotional security. I need relational security. I need to know – to be sure of everything.' And once thought has security, that provides for the endorphins to coat the pain nerves and you feel good. But as soon as that's questioned, the endorphins are removed and the nerves get all excited and there is a drive to think the thoughts that will give you security, saying 'I know it *all*'. That's part of the reflex system.

Therefore, can we stay with the fact that thought does not know it all? There is always uncertainty, at least as far as we can see. There is always the unknown. Our representations are adequate only up to a point.

For instance, a circular table looks like an ellipse from various directions. But we know that those are all different appearances of a single circular form. So we represent the table as a circle. We say 'that's what it is, a solid circle'. But then scientists come along and say 'That's mostly empty space; it is atoms moving around. It's really quite different from the solid circular object it appears to be. It's only very roughly a circle. A cloud might look like a circle, but it's not.' Thus according to these scientists the essence is now the atoms; the circle is only an appearance. But then, ideas about the atom itself have changed over the years. Originally, the word 'atom' meant something that couldn't be cut. Then later physicists said an atom is made of electrons and protons and neutrons and mostly empty space – the atom is only an appearance and these other particles are the essence. And then came quarks. And then came other things.

You could wonder if they are ever going to finish this, or whether it's always just a representation – which may be adequate or not. That is, it may be a correct representation up to a point. If it's correct it will guide us coherently, to the extent that it is correct. But at some stage, since representation is incomplete, it must cease to guide us coherently; and then we need to change our thought.

So we do not expect to find some eternal truth about the nature of matter. The nature of matter as far as we can see could be infinite, unlimited – qualitatively as well as quantitatively. There is no valid reason why we should think of matter as limited. In the nineteenth century people thought that it was limited in one way. In the twentieth century we now have different ideas. And in the twenty-first or the twenty-second they may think entirely differently, and they will look for a new final theory which could be very different from what we have now. And then it might go on and on. But there is no justification for that. It's not the right way to think. To think that way is going to mix up the thought process.

Q: You're saying that knowing can never be absolute?

Bohm: Yes. I've focused on matter where we have the most solid knowledge with science, and that cannot be absolute. And then if we go into society and into the psyche, and so forth, that seems far less definite than the scientific knowledge of matter. Thus we are saying knowledge is limited, because knowledge is only a representation. Knowledge may be adequate, but it is not the thing itself, whatever that may be. It is not 'that which is'.

Q: We could just call it a view, one of many different views.

Bohm: Yes. It's an appearance or a view, but knowledge is also a representation in the sense that you can bring it up again and again. It is a reflex which gives rise to a view.

Q: We have to keep it open, rather than as a closed conclusion.

Bohm: That's right. But then you have to admit that we are not going to get the whole of it – that the unknown is always open. It must be that the unknown is far beyond the known, immensely beyond the known. The point is: *knowledge is limited.* And the proper application of this system of knowledge requires that knowledge know that it is limited.

Q: Are you describing two ways of thinking – one that limits and solidifies and may be practical in a certain way, and another way that is always open?

Bohm: The way that is open is the most practical, because the way that is open includes relative solidification to any degree that may work. We say 'this table is relatively solid, I admit it'. But I don't say 'It's absolutely solid'. You could find an atomic structure in there -it's mostly empty space. If you light a fire, that table turns into gas. The explanation for that is that the atoms are held together by forces, and then when the temperature goes up they just come apart. They go into space.

Therefore, you'd have to say that this table is not absolutely solid. The idea is that it is solid is a representation. I gave the example that it looks solid, you expect it to be solid, your reflexes are set for it to be solid. But if this table were instead a very good laser image, you would be ready to put a glass on it and the glass would go through. And then you would say that the representation was inaccurate.

Q: What is it that allows us to see our conclusions in different areas of life where we are no longer learning, where we've come to an opinion?

Bohm: Opinions may be all right. They are assumptions. We may make assumptions as long as we know that they are assumptions.

Q: But what allows us to see those opinions and those conclusions that we have?

Bohm: I think the question is the other way around. Why *don't* we see them? Why do we think that they are true?

Q: Well, if we tried to programme ourselves to learn about every aspect of ourselves, it seems that would also be just part of the system.

Bohm: You can't do it as a programme. I'm saying there may be an unconditioned capacity or potential in us to look at this and see what it is. That's what I'm suggesting. We leave that open. I think it's essential for healthy thought to leave that open; because if you don't, then you've implied that it's all conditioned and hence there is no way out.

Q: We can't know because of the constant change. We only think we know. There are no absolutes.

Bohm: We never know absolutely. We always can know relatively. It's a fairly good notion that this is a table, it will support objects. I know that. I cannot, however, say the ultimate absolute about it – what it will be like after it changes in time, and so on. Thus we have relative knowledge – relative to certain conditions and circumstances. But the notion that we know the whole thing, or that we have absolute knowledge, will not work.

Also, as you were saying, things change. And knowledge is limited to the past. We extend our knowledge from the past toward the future, we project it. And very often that works. We can make a provisional assumption that what we know is going to work. But the key thing is that it's open. If it doesn't work, then we're ready to see it isn't working and change it.

105

Q: When I look at that table there's a certain 'knowing' of it as a table. But together with that there is a *feeling* of it as a table.

Bohm: Yes, you can feel it. You expect it to be solid, and all the rest.

Q: But within me, together with the representation, comes a feeling of realness.

Bohm: Yes. Reality.

Q: And it seems to me that the feeling is what makes it solid. It's the feeling aspect of the table that locks the doors.

Bohm: But the representation is a set of reflexes all tied together, which includes the feeling and the visual appearance and all that. The word 'table' ties it all together – it stands in for all of that. So now you get a sense that this table is going to be solid, which may be mistaken or may be right.

The mind starts to attribute various qualities to the table, partly according to the way things have gone in the past and partly by what is observed now. There is an example we have used many times. If you see a telephone on a television screen and you hear a ringing noise, then your mind attributes the sound to the telephone in the television image – it seems to be coming from there. That's how you see it. And yet if nobody answers the phone in the image, you then can say that it may be coming from the next room and then you will see it differently. The sense of its being there inside of the television or in the next room comes from the way the thought is working. The set of reflexes can attribute and create the feeling that it is there in the form that is attributed. This is all part of the process.

106

Q: It may be worthwhile to distinguish between 'knowledge' in the past sense and 'knowing'.

Bohm: Knowing requires being open and seeing what is happening now.

Q: You used the example that Einstein was knowing things with his body in a different way. Then knowing isn't just a series of images coming by in some programmed sequence. It can be an extension of being present – which is a form of knowing – not just a series of ideas floating by an observer.

Bohm: Yes. I think you could say that as you get a feeling contact with the table, so Einstein got a feeling contact with the scientific ideas with which he was working, which was part of his thought.

Q: It provided a different kind of barometer for his theories.

Bohm: A richer sort of barometer, yes.

So you have all this representation, which includes all of that: the feeling contact, the visual sense, the sound, the word, and everything else – all the different meanings.

A rainbow is a nice example. Suppose you see a rainbow. It seems to be an object made up of coloured arcs. That's the way you experience it. But according to physics there is no rainbow out there. And in fact, if you assumed that the rainbow was an object and walked toward it, it would not be found. Physics says that there is a bunch of raindrops falling and there is light reflecting off the water and it reaches your eye in a certain way. The light reaches everybody's eye in a rather similar way, therefore everybody agrees there's a rainbow. But this doesn't mean that what is there is a rainbow. What is actually there is falling rain and light refracting – a process.

Q: Isn't that just as true for the table?

Bohm: The difference is that if you walk toward the table you will touch it coherently. If you walk toward the rainbow you will not. So the rainbow is not a coherent object.

Q: It's a sheer image.

Bohm: It's like the holographic image of the ship – it doesn't have the whole being that the ship has. Similarly, the rainbow does not have being as a bow; it has being as a process of falling rain and light refracting. The rainbow is a representation which does not cohere with what it is supposed to represent.

That example is very interesting because it shows the way the thing works. The rainbow is a representation. The representation was probably produced in people even before words. You don't have to have words to have representation, as we've just gone into.

Q: There seems to be a correspondence, however. If you look at the table through a very powerful microscope, in a sense you get closer and closer to the table just as you get closer and closer to the rainbow.

Bohm: But you never get closer to the rainbow. It will move.

Q: There might be some use in pushing that analogy, though, because a table is so real to me in my feeling. But even if I go up and touch it or put a cup on it, all that I finally have is some sort of sensations. And the 'tableness' of it is only in the stepping back and holding something in my mind.

Bohm: Yes. The 'tableness' is built from your mind, out of the whole set of reflexes all tied together. The same is true of everything. Science has said that things come into the nervous system, and it is in the brain that they are somehow built into our sense of the reality of the world. The point is whether this reality coheres in our experience. If the reality that is so formed does not cohere, then we have to change it.

The brain is forming a kind of representation of reality, which is able to guide you properly if it is coherent. And it's clear that this sense of the reality of objects and things is *constructed*. As I said earlier, psychologists such as Piaget claim that very young children may not have the notion of the reality of a permanent object – they may feel that when it is not seen it just vanishes and that something else comes up. For example, he cites the case of a child about two years old who thought that the father who appeared at the dinner table was different from the father in the office; they were two people. Or else they may feel the unity of all objects. So that's part of the thing, whether it is one or many.

That's another abstract concept which you have to get straight in forming the representations. Your representation puts certain things as one, certain things as many, certain things as necessary, contingent, general, particular. It organizes everything. And the meaning is very different according to how it is represented. At first, that child was seeing two fathers. Then he learned there was only one, and therefore he saw only one. Perhaps he discovered the incoherence in seeing two.

Thus, we have to say that representations can be correct up to a point. Appearances can be correct up to a point, or they may be illusory. That distinction is very important. The fact that the brain constructs appearances is not the whole story; but that some of them are correct up to a point is crucial.

Q: Would you say then that the world we see is just a description?

Bohm: No. The description means the way we put it in words; literally it means 'writing it down'. The world we see is far more than those words, but it is organized through a representation in which those words have had a big effect. The way we talk about things and the way we think about things affects how we see them. Whether we see two fathers or one is a crucial point. For instance, if you have printed words which are a bit too far away to be seen and somebody tells you what the words are, you actually see them. There are many examples of that kind – how the word or the thought affects what you see.

This is the point I want to make: *thought is affecting what you see.* The representation enters into the perception. Sometimes you know something is a representation – such as when you draw a diagram or have a photograph. But in many subtle ways the representation enters directly into the perception, and you may miss the fact that it is coming from thought. When you have the representation of somebody as an enemy, that goes into the perception of that person as the enemy, or as stupid, or as whatever.

Q: Is thought a mediation system, which allows us to be aware of things that are not now or not present?

Bohm: Yes, but it is projected into what is now and present. And that projection may be a good guide, it may be accurate; it's approximate, but it may be good enough. In other words, to be useful in what you are doing it is actually important to project that – it is important to see this table as a table, and not to say this is just a representation. When you are going to act toward it, you have to act toward it as something that is present. A lot of it is projected into what is present, but you act toward that too – the only point being that if it is not coherent, you change it.

Therefore it's crucial to see this: *the representation affects the perception.* That is crucial. And it is a tremendous source of illusion if we once lose track of the fact that this is happening.

Q: Does anything have multiple representations?

Bohm: Many things have, yes.

Q: Is there anything that doesn't?

Bohm: I shouldn't think so. You could represent things in many many ways. Thought is unlimited.

Q: We often get locked onto a particular representation.

Bohm: We get locked on a particular one because it may include reflexes that give rise to good chemical states of the endorphins. Also there are other reasons, such as the lock of absolute necessary. There are various factors which can lock this thing so that you can't let it change in the way that is called for when there is incoherence. And that's the way illusion arises, and mistakes arise that you don't correct, and all the rest of that.

Q: Did you say thought is unlimited?

Bohm: There is no limit to how far you can extend thought, saying: 'Now we can grasp this. Tomorrow we could grasp more. We could go on indefinitely.' But each thought is limited. Thought is limited in what it can grasp. Thought does not grasp the whole.

Q: Then it's quite crucial that we check the representation?

Bohm: Yes. What is missing is that we have to be able to see that thought is actually participating in perception. One of the assumptions thought has come to make is that certain kinds of thought do not participate – they only tell you the way things are, or perhaps they represent the way things are.

Now, the point is that thought actually does participate, not only in the fact that we make the world according to thought – our social world, and so on – but also because it participates in the world that we see, either correctly or incorrectly. Thought tells us that the father at the office is the same as the father at the table. But thought does not seem to know that by doing so it is participating – affecting our perception. Not to see that participation is a crucial mistake. Is it clear that this mistake can be very dangerous?

Q: My experience of my representation is my experience of reality, isn't it?

Bohm: The experience of reality includes the projection of representations into what you see. But it is not entirely that, because if your mind is working right you have to take into account that the whole thing is incoherent. Then it loses its hold and you begin to change. Is that clear?

Q: So it is vital that we see the whole thing even beyond the personal. Take the media, for example; they could make you go to war.

Bohm: The media are full of representations which are presented as perceptions. In fact, now they even have docudramas; they're doing it directly. They put something in the form of a documentary which is only a drama.

Q: Could you give an example of a case where representation affects experience and we can see that easily?

Bohm: There are a lot of examples. For instance, very often cartoonists represent certain people as nasty and unpleasant.

Or the Nazis would represent the Jews in a certain way, and then soon people were seeing them that way.

Q: But I meant more like from our tangible everyday experience where we could see how it works.

Bohm: This is what we're trying to get to. It is a very subtle question. To see this thing actually happening is something the human race doesn't do.

However, there are a lot of examples of how representation affects perception. I gave the one of where you have an indistinct letter and somebody states what it is and you then see it that way. If, on the other hand, the figure is distinct, then you cannot easily see the effect of representation. But in an ambiguous situation it becomes clear that the way you are thinking is affecting the way you see. There are hundreds of examples of that kind.

Q: And you're suggesting that this is actually the general case, although we may think it is an exception.

Bohm: Yes. I'm saying that is the way perception works – it is highly affected by thought and by representation and by imagination, and so on. And in fact, that is quite inevitable. But we do not seem to see this happening.

There are historians who say that in very early times people had a more participatory type of thought. They would think that they were participating in some of the things they saw, like saying that they participated in the totem of the tribe or in the whole of nature. And the Eskimos apparently had a belief that there were many many seals, but that each one was a manifestation of the one seal – the spirit of the seal. That is, the one seal was manifesting as the many. Therefore, they could pray to this spirit of the seal to manifest so they could have something to eat. Now, if you thought all seals were individuals, that prayer would be ridiculous because

113

you are asking this individual seal just to come and be eaten. But to the spirit of the seal it would be 'but of course, I'll just manifest for the Eskimos and I'll still be here'. I think that the American Indians looked at the buffalo that way.

The earlier people felt that they were participating in nature. And in some way they were more keenly aware of the participation of their thought. However, in another way they were perhaps overdoing it – in the sense that they were supposing the reality of some of the things which were being projected by the thought, in a way that may not have been entirely right.

Then we developed instead a more objective kind of thought which said; 'we want to have a thought about something where we don't participate, where we just think about it and know just what it is.' That made possible science and technology, and so forth. But that also went too far, because we began to apply that objective thought universally and said it applied inside, outside – to everything. And then we say there is no participation whatsoever by thought.

Now, that is clearly wrong. I've pointed out that there is a great deal of participation by thought, and how it creates the world. And I'm saying also that thought clearly participates in perception, and that that is the crucial form of participation. Thought participates in everything; but our ideal of objective thought is absolute non-participation – the idea that thought is just simply telling you the way things are and doing nothing whatsoever. In some areas that's a good approximation; but our thought has supposed that to be the universal situation.

Thus, we could say that here is one of the questions where thought is going wrong. And this could be said to be very close to the fundamental flaw in the process – namely, that thought is doing this thing and doesn't realize that it's doing it. Is it clear what the question is?

Q: This may sound simplistic, but are you saying that thought can only function by dividing; and once it's divided, it can't be the whole?

Bohm: Thought cannot be the whole because it is just a representation, an abstraction.

But also, there is a difference between dividing and fragmenting. Thought may divide in the sense of marking parts of a whole – such as distinguishing the various gears of a watch. Or thought may fragment – such as smashing the watch with a hammer. In the latter case, thought separates things which are really one. You see, we ought to make just a dotted line between thought and perception. But thought has tacitly made a separation rather than marking parts of a whole. Thought has made a solid line and says thought is one side and perception is on the other.

Q: And that line has this physiological component, and so the line is experienced as real.

Bohm: Yes. The separation, the division, is experienced as real – that's the representation of thought. That becomes the perception of the situation.

Q: Are you saying that thought, by setting boundaries, is creating a separation all the time?

Bohm: It is creating the sense of separation, and then the action flowing from that breaks things up. We'll have to discuss this some more. But this is really getting close the crucial difficulty with thought – that it does not keep track of what it is doing. That has been the difficulty all along.

Q: Thought is making a representation and presenting it as a perception?

115

Bohm: Yes.

Q: But that's a deception.

Bohm: No, it's not necessarily one, because it may be necessary for practical purposes to see this table as a table. If you are driving a car, you haven't time to go through all those thoughts. You must directly move towards what you see, which includes a lot of thought. The meaning of what you see is included in how you see it, so it is a necessary feature of the whole system.

And yet, if thought knew it was doing this, then it would be all right. The deception consists in the fact that thought doesn't know it is doing it.

Q: Then it isn't that *I* am doing it, but thought is doing it.

Bohm: Yes, thought is doing it. But it doesn't even know it is happening. It says: 'That's perception, I'm thought. I'm just telling you the way things are. I see the way things are and I just tell you.'

Q: There's a complete separation between me and what is happening.

Bohm: That's right. A separation which is false, because the way I think is affecting what I see.

Q: So that perception of the 'me' as separate is wrong?

Bohm: I don't think that we've got to the 'me' yet. We are just trying to say there is a mistake in thought, even before we raise the question of 'me'. Now, that mistake in thought will allow this false notion of the 'me' to develop.

116

I think we should have a break now.

Bohm: We were talking about how thought affects perception and doesn't know that it does so. And we said that this could be a crucial mistake, because if we don't see how thought enters perception we may take that perception as a fact unaffected by thought, and then base our assumptions and actions and thinking on that so-called fact. Thus we can get into a trap – such as we may assume that people of a certain kind are no good, and then say 'I can *see* that they're no good'.

We said that this question of thought entering perception requires some attention, because it will not only do so outwardly but also inwardly. And we will have to see the serious consequences of that when we consider whether it is possible to perceive ourselves and to disentangle the confusion from our thoughts about ourselves.

Now, maybe you want to ask one or two more questions and then we'll go on.

Q: You talked earlier about how very deceptive thought can be, and then you also talked about how unaware thought can be. Somehow I get the feeling of a very coy and conniving thought.

Bohm: In a way thought is very cunning. But it's not really very aware of what it is doing. The same cunning is also what solves practical problems. We can think of thought as a set of reflexes which has tremendous adaptability. It can, for example, find all sorts of ways of making you feel better. It feels around, it probes, it finds ways which may look extremely ingenious. But that doesn't mean that thought has really a vicious spirit there trying to do you wrong, or do you in or something.

Q: There is a kind of wishful thinking that supports the weakness of the memory, the forgetfulness of certain details.

Bohm: Yes, part of the deception of thought may include the fact that it makes you forget. Thought is able to make you insensitive to all the reflexes which might make you sleepy or not, or inattentive, or forgetful or whatever. Thought can take command of those reflexes and operate them. For instance, if the body has too much of the chemical serotonin it could make you a bit dopey. So thought might find a way to liberate serotonin by certain thoughts. Thought can probe around. It's one system, all of it.

That's the crucial point: that it is all thought, and all those movements are all one system. The system even enters perception, and it affects perception. Thought could make you feel sleepy, thought could make you feel very excited, or thought could make the mind dart so that it won't stay with the point, saying 'quick, something else is important'. It can do all sorts of tricks to try to keep your mind off a point that thought supposes might be disturbing.

Q: Do you think that thought is basically doing it to be helpful? It's not really doing it for any other reason?

Bohm: Yes, it's doing what it is supposed to do – to try to help. But it's extremely confused about what it is doing. So it often does harm.

Q: It doesn't seem, though, that thought has the whole system's well-being as its aim or goal; it seems that it's much more a particular pleasure or sensation.

Bohm: But that's the way thought conceives the key feature of the whole system, getting that pleasure or pain. Originally thought was set up to try to protect you and to help you. And after a while it runs on its own. And it's just running. I don't think you should think it is trying to do anything, any more than your knee-jerk is trying to do anything.

Q: But we can see that, in many cases at least, thought is trying to achieve a certain objective – pleasure or satisfaction, whatever that means.

Bohm: That's the way you interpret it, but thought may not be doing that. Suppose the endorphins have suddenly been removed from the pain nerves, and the brain is objecting very strongly. Thought merely reacts, it responds with reflexes aimed at doing whatever will reduce that – which is what it does all the time anyway.

Q: It's more of a mechanical view than we would like to admit.

Bohm: Yes. I'm trying to say that these reflexes are relatively mechanical. And, though the brain as a whole is not mechanical, it can get caught up into a system of reflexes that looks like a machine.

Q: Isn't it that the brain demands security?

Bohm: That's right. But faced with some sort of disturbance the brain gets agitated, and the thought process comes in with reflexes to try to diminish the agitation. There is nothing special about it. Thought just goes on as if it were a machine, though it is not a machine.

Q: After the fact, we call it these things. We say that it's trying to do something or that it's mechanical. But that's only a description after the fact. Within the fact itself there is merely what is going on.

Bohm: Yes, in effect it's behaviour can be represented as mechanical, but only up to a point.

119

Q: Can you clarify for me what you understand by psychic energy and thought, and the connection between both of them.

Bohm: Thought will liberate through the reflexes all sorts of energies. Thought is in command, as it were, of a whole range of energies, which in turn affect thought. These energies are not the most subtle energies of the unconditioned, but there are a great range of energies there.

Q: Isn't thought primarily dominated by conditioning, but we do have a small percentage there where we have the opportunity to see things differently? And the new conditioning comes out of that, and then there is a change?

Bohm: That's right. Thought works by conditioning. It has to get conditioned. You need conditioning to learn a language, to learn how to write, or to do all sorts of things. When the conditioning gets too rigid, though, it won't change when it should. But there may be areas where it is not that rigid and it could change, and then you can get something new – a new set of reflexes.

Q: But there's a window of opportunity occasionally where we see something. That's the reason we sometimes get an insight to change.

Bohm: Yes. The window may arise in all sorts of fortuitous ways, or perhaps non-fortuitous. What we are doing now is, I hope, creating some kind of window. In other words, perhaps the unconditioned energy is awakening, or something, and therefore it can begin to look at this conditioning.

Q: When there's the disappearance of the endorphins and

then the agitation of the brain to get that state back, what are the other possibilities besides what thought does?

Bohm: If thought didn't do anything, it might be that another solution would come. The agitation might just disappear. It may be that if you stay with the fact that there are no endorphins for a little while, the system will soon come to an equilibrium. There may be no real problem at all except that thought says 'quick, I must do something'.

Let me say a few more points here. We have this question of thought affecting perception. This will be very crucial tomorrow when we discuss the thought and the thinker or the observer and the observed, or whatever you want to call it, because the question arises: if thought affects what we perceive, how are we going to separate the two?

We have with the body a very interesting situation called *proprioception*, which means 'self-perception'. If you move any part of your body, you know that you have moved it – the movement resulted from your intention. You know that immediately, without time, without an observer, without having to think. If you can't tell that, then you're in a very bad way. There are people who have lost it and they can't move coherently, because you must be able to distinguish between a movement that you have created and one that occurred independently.

I've often cited the case of a woman who woke up in the middle of the night hitting herself. What had happened was that she'd had a stroke that damaged her sensory nerves, which would tell her what she was doing. But the stroke left the motor nerves so that she could still move her muscles. Apparently she had touched herself, but since she wasn't being informed that it was her own touch she assumed right away that it was an attack by somebody else. Then the more she defended the worse the attack got. When the light was turned on, the proprioception was reestablished because she could then see with her eyes what she was doing, so she stopped hitting herself. There was also a case published of another woman who somehow lost proprioception over-night, and couldn't move her body without watching every movement. She had to learn to watch very skilfully and somehow to get along; apparently that never changed.

Normally this quality of proprioception exists for the body. And one of the things we need to see is the relation between the intention to move and the movement – to see immediately that relation, to be aware of it. We're usually not very aware of this intention to move, but we can be. If somebody wants to make his movements more accurate or skilled he will find his intention is not that well defined – he doesn't move the way he hopes. Somebody who wants to play the piano, for instance, has to learn that relation better so that his fingers will do what he wants them to do. So a greater quality of proprioception occurs in that regard.

The essence of the movement may be in the intention to move, which unfolds into the whole movement. For example, we knew of a man who had a degenerative disease and was unable to move at all. He could barely talk. And yet he taught movement in a university. The question is how he could do it. You could guess that, being very intelligent and unable to move, he was somehow much more aware of the intention than we are, because we focus our attention on the result. Therefore, getting the intention right may be very crucial to making the movement right. Thus there is some relation between the intention to move and the movement; and there is something in between that you are vaguely aware of, which is proprioception.

There is one point I would like to bring up now which is related to this. I'm going to say that thought is a movement – every reflex is a movement really. It moves from one thing to another. It may move the body or the chemistry or just simply the image or something else. So when 'A' happens 'B' follows. It's a movement.

All these reflexes are interconnected in one system, and the suggestion is that they are not in fact all that different. The intellectual part of thought is more subtle, but actually all the reflexes are basically similar in structure. Hence, we should think of thought as a part of the bodily movement, at least explore that possibility, because our culture has led us to believe that thought and bodily movement are really two totally different spheres which are not basically connected. But maybe they are not different. The evidence is that thought is intimately connected with the whole system.

If we say that thought is a reflex like any other muscular reflex – just a lot more subtle and more complex and changeable – then we ought to be able to be proprioceptive with thought. Thought should be able to perceive its own movement, be aware of its own movement. In the process of thought there should be awareness of that movement, of the intention to think and of the result which that thinking produces. By being more attentive, we can be aware of how thought produces a result outside ourselves. And then maybe we could also be attentive to the results it produces within ourselves. Perhaps we could even be immediately aware of how it affects perception. It has to be immediate, or else we will never get it clear. If you took time to be aware of this, you would be bringing in the reflexes again. So is such proprioception possible? I'm raising that question. Is it clear what the question means?

Q: Do 'we' have to be aware? Or could you say that there may be an awareness; and then after that moment of awareness some thought may be made about it?

Bohm: Can the movement of the body be aware of itself proprioceptively? You could ask that question. The movement of the body includes all that goes with it – the awareness and everything. A movement without awareness is quite different from a movement with. So could we also say, 'can the movement of thought be aware of itself?'.

Q: Can you distinguish that from self-consciousness?

Bohm: Yes, because when you move the body and are aware

of it you are not self-conscious. If you were it wouldn't work. You may even be very busy thinking about something else, but you are aware if you have moved your body. Whatever you are doing, you take directly into account whether you have produced that movement, and you act accordingly. Suppose you push on something and it moves. You know immediately that you moved it. That's different from thinking that it suddenly moved by itself. You are aware of it, and you don't have to be thinking about yourself. That sort of awareness is also necessary for you to be able to walk properly, or whatever.

This whole movement is somehow aware of the relation between the intention and the result, because you say: 'That is a result of my intention to move and this other is not. This came from somewhere else.' But you don't put that in words or go through a complicated analysis or anything. You are somehow directly aware, and then all the reflexes can behave accordingly. Is that clear?

Now, suppose thought could do this. I've given an argument saying why it should be able to do it. If thought is just an extension of all those body reflexes, maybe thought could be directly aware of its movement, and then could be aware of what it is doing. The basic trouble with thought now is that it participates and is not aware of how it is participating.

Q: May we go back to the physical? I didn't understand what was meant by 'self-conscious'. I wouldn't put the self into it, but rather I would say that you actually have to be with that movement or with that sensation at that moment.

Bohm: Yes, but you're not aware of yourself thinking and being separate from the movement. When you say 'I am thinking about myself', you begin to get into that sort of thing.

If thought tried to look at itself in the usual way, by separating itself from itself, then it couldn't do it. But suppose thought, without separating itself in any way, would just be

124

aware that it is moving. And various things are happening, including things outside and things happening inside – not only feelings and things like that, but also perceptions are being affected, and so on. Could we be aware – immediately see it – that *this* change of perception came through thought and *that* change of perception came because the object actually changed? This is important.

I may perceive that you suddenly became angry at me. That may happen because you actually became angry. But I could also have suddenly thought of something which made me see you as angry – that's paranoia. Suppose, for example, the boss is walking along with a nondescript look on his face. I look at him and think: 'He's unhappy and frowning. Maybe he is thinking he's going to fire me.' So I see him as ready to fire me. That came from my perception being affected by thought. On the other hand, maybe he is actually ready to fire me. The distinction is very important. And you may even help to make it happen by seeing it wrongly, because you will behave in a way which will induce him to want to do it.

We are usually able to get some of those questions straight about how thought affects perception, saying 'OK, that's just my imagination'. But very often we don't. Paranoia is a case where proprioception has failed still more, and people have a much harder time getting it straight, if at all. The paranoid person can't tell the difference between what he has done and what has happened independently. He sees threats everywhere, which may be his own thoughts. He projects his own fears, and so forth, into his perceptions all the time. People are doing that anyway, but in paranoia it gets exaggerated beyond what people usually do and such people become unable to function.

Q: When something happens like a boss is walking down the hall with a particular expression on his face, that may be just a perceptual fact. But any interpretation on that has to be questioned.

125

Bohm: But the difficulty is that you don't see it as an interpretation, especially if you are paranoid. The thought or the interpretation that you had, which is a representation of a boss who is ready to fire you, becomes the *perception* of the boss who is ready to fire you.

Q: Don't we all do that?

Bohm: We all do it but to different degrees. Paranoia is merely exaggeration of the usual behaviour. It goes too far.

Q: Is it like leprosy in thought? Yesterday you talked about leprosy as if it was some problem with proprioception.

Bohm: It is in a way. With leprosy, the nerves which will tell the muscles what they are doing have been damaged and they don't feel the pain which you should feel when you over-exert. And therefore you may pull the whole nose out of joint. You may pull your fingers off. You may destroy everything because you are not being informed properly of the force you are using. And then when you see the limbs coming off or the fingers coming off you say 'my God, the fingers are coming off by themselves'. But you're actually pulling them off without noticing.

Q: Doesn't paranoia have qualities like that?

Bohm: It does. For example, if somebody treats a person as an enemy or as a threat then it will become visible and that person may become frightened and respond.

Q: Are all representations within the system? Could there be a form of representation of another dimension?

126

Bohm: The system produces representations. In so far as they are based on the past, they are in the system.

Q: The way we function now, the brain is not proprioceptive?

Bohm: It is in many ways, but not in this way – not in thought.

Q: Are you suggesting that it may be possible to function in a mode that acts as if there were proprioception?

Bohm: Or where there, in fact, would be proprioception. I'm saying that from the argument I've given, I don't see why I should distinguish what goes on in the brain from what goes on anywhere in the body, or what goes on in thought from what goes on with the muscles, or with anything. They are all basically similar, though different in many ways.

Q: Does the lack of proprioception in thought as we now know it mean that I cannot distinguish whether an image is based on that which is going on or on what I think is going on?

Bohm: That's right. We should be able to say: 'I see what is going on. I have formed inferences. I distinguish my inferences from what I see. And I will check my inferences against what I see later. But my seeing is not confused with the inferences.' That would be common sense, clear thinking. But now that is blocked by the fact that some of the things I 'see' have actually been projected by my thought or my representations. And then when I start thinking about them, I'm thinking about them wrongly. They are conclusions. As they say in the court, they are conclusions and not facts. But they look like facts.

127

Q: And sometimes what we perceive is terrifying. But it may be actually that the *way* we perceive is terrifying.

Bohm: Yes, we are projecting terrible things. When you are dreaming you may project terrible things into the dream. It's the same sort of thing. What you perceive in a dream may be entirely due to thought, but it is quite convincing as a perception.

Q: What I meant was that if we had proprioception, probably the first thing we would notice is that there is something terrifying actually going on, which is the way we see things. The way the thought is working is dangerous.

Bohm: Or perhaps if there were proprioception we wouldn't go on with this insane way of perceiving.

Q: In order for it to occur, one would have to have no censoring of whatever came up. And that's very painful and difficult.

Bohm: But what tells you that it is painful and difficult is part of the thought process. The pain may come from the same system which is causing all the rest of the trouble. The thought process says 'that's going to be very painful and difficult'. And therefore you will feel it, just as you feel the reality of the table.

Q: Are you saying then, that the human species doesn't know what it does and doesn't know how it perceives, and that there might be another way of seeing?

Bohm: Yes. Therefore the first thing is that thought itself must change in some way. I would like to give an image or an analogy. I want to say that thought takes itself as very big. But maybe it's just a ripple on the stream. And the stream is the stream of consciousness. So the stream of consciousness has to be aware of itself. But that's no great thing because consciousness is simply allowed to be aware. The question is: can the stream of consciousness be proprioceptively aware of this ripple that it is producing, just as it is aware of how it moves the body?

Q: That's somehow addressing the difficulty I've been having about understanding how thought could be aware of itself. It seems to make perfect sense when you describe it. But I have some notion that thought, being memory, can only describe; it can't be aware.

Bohm: But thought is also more.

Q: That's what I mean. You use the phrase 'the movement of thought being aware of itself'.

Bohm: In a sense, memory is more than just memory, because memory is a set of reflexes. It's a movement. What memory actually is, is movement. The word 'memory' usually represents something just stored up. But memory is also a movement in the brain. And memory, which is abstraction, is a representation of something which is itself not abstract.

Q: If memory is a movement, then what you call 'conditioning' or the tape-recording of assumptions is also a movement.

Bohm: Yes. But the tape is too mechanical an analogy; I would rather not say 'taped', but 'conditioned'. You can think that each time you do something, it leaves a little bit of change in the nerves so it builds up a pattern. It gets more and more fixed.

129

Q: When you say that thought is like the ripple on the surface of the stream of consciousness, that makes it sound as if in principle it should be very simple and easy to see this ripple.

Bohm: It may be actually, but we don't. Being in this mode of consciousness we are now in, this ripple seems to be everything. It is represented to be everything and therefore perceived as everything.

Q: That might be one of the mistakes – that we think it's more difficult than it may in fact be.

Bohm: That may be so. We can't count on what thought tells us about how difficult it is. Thought doesn't really know. So it's best to say that we don't know how difficult it is; and to say that whatever thought says about this, it doesn't really know.

Q: This thing of proprioception functioning in the thought process – the thought being aware of itself – can you approach that in some different way?

Bohm: Well, thought is now conditioned to the representation of itself in various ways: that it is different from the body, that it doesn't affect perception, that it's just telling you the way things are, and so on. And therefore, that is the way you perceive how thought works. Whatever thought represents can become how you perceive it. Now, 'outside' you have a check for your perceptions. If you perceive this as a cup when it is something else, you will soon find out by sensory experience that that is incoherent. So perceptions which are mistaken show up as incoherence and we correct them. But 'inside' it is much harder, because you can't get hold of it. We speak of thought as being inside; it isn't really, because it is also the whole world.

Thought presents itself as separate from perception, as just telling you the way things are. Thought has this picture of how it works – that you see certain things and then thought merely tells you more about them; that it draws inferences, it does nothing and has no effect. Therefore that's the way you see thought. But thought is actually doing more than that. It is affecting how you perceive everything. Is that clear?

Q: You're saying that the thought-body process is one movement.

Bohm: Yes. And also the perception, the sense perception.

Q: There's also awareness. Awareness must be upstream from all of this.

Bohm: Fundamentally, yes. I'm suggesting that there is available an awareness, a stream of consciousness, which is more fundamental, which I imaged as being in the depth of the ocean. But awareness, too, may be confused with the operation of the system, because the system can make a representation of awareness and then take the representation to be that fundamental consciousness itself.

We say thought is a representation, it's a form. A representation is always a certain form. The rainbow is a certain form. The letters are a certain form. The artist makes a form. A representation is always a form; but that form then becomes, apparently, a part of 'what is'. Now, everybody can see that a representation is hardly more than a ripple; it doesn't have much substance – anybody can see that. But when it fuses with perception, then it seems to have all the substance.

Q: The representation is an abstraction, it's a symbol which also has its physical components.

131

Bohm: It has, but as a physical thing it is very, very tiny. I mean, it may be only a few bits of ink on paper, or some little electric current in the brain.

Q: It does not have a structure?

Bohm: It has a structure. The form has a structure, but it has no independent substance. It has no inherent internal necessity.

Q: Could you represent it as the surface, with something more subtle underneath?

Bohm: Yes. When you look at the surface of the ocean, all sorts of *forms* will appear on those waves. They change this way and that way and the other way. There's very little to hold them. There is very little in it. And then you have the depth.

Those forms, however, have a meaning in the mind. And everything follows according to that meaning – it has to. But an important part of the meaning is wrong, because one part is missing: namely, it should mean that that is only an outward form on the surface. But instead it means that that form is the basic substance of 'what is'.

Q: Does that imply that there are two kinds of perception – one superficial and one of essence?

Bohm: I'm saying that there may be a deeper perception, one which starts from these depths. But what we ordinarily take to be perception – or at least what thought takes to be perception, which we ordinarily call 'perception' – is highly affected by thought. Certainly, our ordinary sense perception is generally of that nature, though it may perhaps occasionally get out of it.

At this moment we only have to worry about what thought is taking as the source of its information. Now, thought takes sense perception, among other things, as the source of its information; and it says that sense perception is unaffected by thought – that it is just telling you something. And thought will then proceed from there. But it may turn out that the perception has already been affected by thought, and that thought is thus taking something it has done as being a fact independent of thought.

Q: Which prevents the depth perception?

Bohm: Eventually it muddles the brain up so much that it prevents almost everything. Based on that apparent fact a lot of other things start to happen, and the brain muddles up. From that going wrong, it spreads and becomes a systemic fault. It spreads into everything.

Q: Would you say that there's non-perception of the interference of thought, there's perception of the interference of thought and there's no thought interfering?

Bohm: Yes, those are possible states. Let's suppose that thought is able to be aware of its own effects. Then when it is producing effects which make no sense it would simply stop doing so. Thought is not maliciously trying to destroy everything. It is apparently doing whatever it does according to its own mechanism.

When you have proprioception of the body, you wouldn't make the sort of mistake that you would if you didn't have it – like that woman who got into attacking herself. Similarly, when you don't have proprioceptive thought, you may start attacking yourself, you hurt yourself. You say 'I'm hurt', under the impression that the attack has come from the outside.

Q: You're talking not so much about a way of thinking but a way of perception?

Bohm: Yes, it is some extension of perception. I'm saying that perhaps such an extension of perception is possible.

Q: Would proprioception of thought take place not in what we think of as thought, but actually in the physical, since they are all the same thing?

Bohm: That's actually the case. Since it is all physical it's an extension of the ordinary proprioception into something more subtle, but still of the same general nature. That's the point I'm trying to make; that this distinction between thought and the physical is one where we should just draw a dotted line. But we have drawn a great big gulf between them in our thought. And therefore we perceive them that way.

Q: I wonder if one of the reasons why people ask to have this explained over and over again is that when you say 'thought being aware of its own movement', or, 'proprioception', the thinking makes an image of what that would be. And rather than just listening to what you're saying about thought noticing its activity, thought starts trying to make a description of what it would be like to be aware.

Bohm: Yes. And the difficulty with that description is that it enters your perception. It would be all right to describe it if you said 'frankly this is a speculative attempt to imagine what it might be, but it might not be that at all'. But instead you just represent it in the imagination; and very quickly it spreads over and becomes, apparently, some kind of reality which misleads you. Now, that very process – the thing we just described – is part of the fault in the system. It's just another form of the fault.

Q: What if I'm not able to make much of a description, and I say I can't do this?

Bohm: But then that enters your perception as impossible and therefore you perceive a block. If it's impossible then it is not even necessary to listen. I mean, you don't have to take it seriously at all. The rest follows.

Q: So we're not going to get out of the situation where our representations or thinking have an effect. But rather, we are to be more aware of what's happening in there.

Bohm: Yes. And also to describe it correctly when we do see what is happening; because if we see what is happening and describe it wrongly, we will be misinforming the system about what it is doing, and the system will then get more confused. All the information the system has about itself affects what it does.

It's important to grasp this. Grasping it intellectually, or perhaps a little bit beyond, would be the first step, because this will help clear away a lot of the confusion. But as long as you are tacitly accepting all the other ideas about this process you are going to see it that way, and you will never get into it. Is it clear what I mean?

So it's very important to draw correct inferences about thought. These are not mere idle speculations; rather, we have been observing and then drawing inferences, and then trying to test them as far as we can or see whether we feel they are reasonable. This is just a kind of extension of common sense, when it is used properly. It's the way you observe something – you draw inferences from it; you then look again and see whether your inferences are correct, coherent, and so on.

This is the way we're going – we are proceeding by inference. But as we said before, this is not enough because it still won't get rid of the reflexes. However, it is a useful step. Whether it is necessary I can't say, but I think that to be able to clear up some of this confusion, which has been in the previous set of assumptions and ideas that the system has about itself, will be an important step.

Q: Would it be possible for a person to describe the proprioceptive process in thought as it actually functions?

Bohm: Perhaps a little later. Anything that you have seen might be given a correct description. But if you haven't yet seen it, then it becomes fanciful and it starts entering the other way – it affects your perception as if you had seen it.

Q: The question seems to be: how are we going to bring forward that subtlety, so we can start dissipating this gross abnormality of thought that doesn't see itself working and operating?

Bohm: When you use the word 'how', that can be taken to mean 'by what system will I do it?', or 'how will the system do it?'.

Q: What would you propose, then?

Bohm: We're saying that for the time being you can just consider the question. The attempt to regard this as solving a problem is going to get in the way, isn't it? That problem-solving attitude is all right in a certain area where the system works. But somehow we have to have another approach in this area.

Q: If thought is from the past experiences and projected to the future, would it be that if we're in the present we can see this thought process working?

Bohm: That may well be. But then you have the question of how we get into the present. Or, why aren't we in the present? Obviously we must be in the present. Where else could we be? But why don't we see this? We don't live in the past. Some people are said to live in the past, but that's only a figure of speech; you don't address letters to them into the past. The question is then: why are we not seeing that we live in the present, if it is in fact true?

So you can see that this is the way the system is working. And there are other features of this system which need going into. It will require that we also go into the question of *time*. The system also contains the whole system of time, as well as the system of the self and the observer and the observed.

But I think we have begun to see enough of it to see that there *might* be a way out – not to say there is, but there might be. Now, this requires that we see thought as one whole, with the entire chemical-physical system, and all that.

Q: Is proprioception something different from representing?

Bohm: Yes, clearly. When you have proprioception of the arm you don't represent the arm to yourself in any way. You are just simply directly aware – you're not thinking, representing the arm and how it is moving.

Q: But is anything perceiving anything else?

Bohm: No. I'm trying to say that we have part of our language which says that if anything is perceived there must be something else to perceive it. But that may not be so, and that may be getting in the way. Why can't we say that the stream of consciousness can be aware of itself, or that we don't need a separate perceiver to perceive?

Q: Wouldn't it be hard for this consciousness to be only physical Newtonian matter?

137

Bohm: We're not saying it is just physical Newtonian matter. I said before, I think, that matter may be unlimited in its subtlety. In other words, part of the trouble with our thought is that it says matter is very limited, that it is only this or that or the other – which wouldn't be able to do this sort of thing at all. However, that would suggest that we already know everything about matter. But I'm saying it is crucial to say that we *don't* know everything about matter.

Q: Then are you suggesting that matter can perceive?

Bohm: We haven't come to that yet, but matter is capable of something far more subtle than we might think. At the very least it is going to respond to perception in new ways. For example, a new perception might begin to change some of the synapses, or these things that are rigidly stuck. And so on. We'll come to that later.

Q: You said earlier that the body obviously has proprioception and thought seems to be lacking it; and since the body and thought processes are only separated by a dotted line, thought, at some level, would have to have the movement of proprioception in its nature. However, some shocks or noise or something else happening in thought is drowning out sensitivity to this movement.

Bohm: Yes. Something is happening in thought which rejects sensitivity or prevents it or resists it. It's clear that if you could see the activity of thought, you might discover that most of the things we're counting on actually are just nothing; they are produced by thought – the self and the society, and on and on.

Q: When we perceive with proprioception, are we perceiving directly what is?

138

Bohm: The movement, as it is, is somehow perceiving itself.

Q: When we perceive without proprioception we are perceiving from memory?

Bohm: From the reflexes of memory, right.

Q: So there is a possibility of something more direct?

Bohm: Yes. Memory is not adequate for perceiving the movement of thought. That seems clear, because memory will never perceive the immediate, direct movement of thought.

Q: I've seen a lot of my friends who are interested in this. And it seems that they are more and more muddled and theoretical and inhibited, and almost start to lose a certain amount of common sense in dealing with life. They become so caught up trying to be aware of themselves that it makes me cautious. Am I going to start getting all muddled and anxious and stop living because I'm so worried about being aware of myself?

Bohm: I'm not suggesting that you do that.

The first point is if you just look at yourself without understanding the questions we've been raising you will be looking at something which you have invented by thought. And you will get muddled, inevitably. I'm explaining why you do get muddled when you just simply engage in introspection – because whatever you see has been produced by thought, and is presented as perception. Therefore, what you are seeing is just a lot of forms and clouds and will-o'-the-wisps, and so on.

Q: You don't strike me as muddled at all. But I'm trying to understand what it takes to do this.

Bohm: Perhaps you have an assumption that whoever looks at this is going to get muddled, which is an assumption of necessity.

Q: I'm trying to understand what it is that determines if you get muddled or not.

Bohm: But the fact that you raised the question suggests to me that there is some assumption underneath it.

Q: That does happen often.

Bohm: That's the way we build these assumptions. When something happens often, we say that it will happen always, that it is necessary – it is always necessary. And we get stuck. That's the sort of thing we slip into. It may happen very frequently, but that doesn't mean always. Once again, we have to say that we don't know everything about it and therefore we can't say it happens always. Now, that's the first point.

Then the second point is, as we've explained: if you don't look into these questions, such as proprioception and some of the others, you are surely going to get muddled. I mean, from the explanation I've given it becomes inevitable that exactly the experience you describe is going to happen. So that explains your experience.

The third point is: it's not as if everything is going to be all right if we don't look into this. We are then going to continue to have this muddle going on in the world, which will lead ultimately to heaven knows what. We don't even know what it is going to do in the relatively near future, because it could lead to some pretty disastrous things. It's not as if you could say: 'Well, leave this alone and everything is going to be all right. We're going to have nice common sense.' Because common sense has broken down in the face of this. It's not that common sense is wrong, but you cannot carry out common sense when all this is going on.

Therefore I would say that you have to look at it very carefully and think very carefully. It's true that there are all the dangers you say. But there are also dangers in not doing it. Then what will we do with that? It seems to me that generally it would be reasonable to say all the several alternatives are dangerous. But one of them is almost surely going to fail – namely, what is going on now. And this other may have some possibility of working.

I think that what I've said gives a coherent explanation of the various phenomena which are actually happening. That's one of the things that it does. And all the times you find that it isn't working it explains why it isn't working, which mean we still have a challenge – we haven't got to the bottom, to the end of it.

Q: What did you mean by 'we still have a challenge'?

Bohm: We have gone so far, explained all these things, but we have not touched the reflexes sufficiently. We have had some effect on them, probably. But these reflexes will still operate.

Q: The explanation isn't doing it.

Bohm: Yes. The explanation is useful, it is necessary, but something more is needed.

Q: And you think it's reasonable to assume that the phenomena are there, and the explanation is correct as far as we've gone?

Bohm: Let's just say that as far as we can see up to now the explanation is correct, that we have gone through this thing by careful observation and inference and testing and it all seems reasonable. Anybody who thought it wasn't reasonable had a chance to say so. And so far we can't find a hole in it. It does explain all these cases, all these different difficulties that arise. It explains them. They are to be expected within this thing, and we are not to be surprised by them.

Q: Can we discuss the present a little more? Thought is conditioned by the past and it projects what's going to happen in the future; so I'm missing what is happening in the present because my mind is conditioned to what has happened, or to what is going to happen. Whereas if I'm in the present, I'm actually hearing everything that's going on – the people around me, or whatever happens – and at the same time I'm listening to what you are saying and I'm also listening to how my body feels. It's one movement. There is no separation; I'm one with you. And being in that state of presence I can watch my thoughts.

Bohm: And what happens then?

Q: By watching my thoughts I release their hold on me. It's as though they are moving and I'm watching them, I'm not caught up in them. By watching them I'm not them, so I can question what they are telling me.

Bohm: But if you say 'I'm watching', then somebody could ask: 'Who's watching? Is there a separation?'

Q: I don't think we can say 'I am watching'. There is just watching, because 'I' and thought are together, not separated. It's a kind of deception to say that I am watching.

Bohm: Perhaps we'll try to go into that further tomorrow. But I think that to change this we need a kind of insight

142

that will change this physical situation, this physical-chemical situation.

Q: Is there value in the objective of trying to describe such an insight, rather than somehow challenging ourselves to have it?

Bohm: When you have it you could say something about it. The question is to say something that will actually communicate what it is.

Q: And also, it seems we may sometimes be able to watch our thoughts and talk about it. But when the emotions kick in then we lose that ability; something else comes in.

Bohm: We have to have this thing so powerful and firm that it works even when the emotions do come in. And the ability to watch what is happening in thought may be moving to give rise to perception.

We can say that there has to be a real change to make this thing work. There has to be a change in this conditioning, in this material base of the conditioning, so that it doesn't hold so strongly. And I think that that requires an insight.

The time is getting late now, so we might want to discuss this tomorrow.

Q: Could you give us something to do as a little homework for tonight?

Bohm: I think the best thing would be to do what we were discussing this morning. That is, to try to use the words which bring up the process – not only with anger or fear or jealousy or even pleasure, but with whatever may be there.

Q: How about resistance?

143

Bohm: If you have resistance, then the point is to try to find the thought and use the word that is behind the resistance. You find the words which are behind it. If you want to do an exercise then that would be a good one to try.

Q: Would you recommend discussing it with somebody or writing it down?

Bohm: You could write it down for yourself as a diary. Or if you want you could discuss with somebody. Whatever way you find convenient.

SUNDAY MORNING

Bohm: We've discussed a number of things and there are still quite a few to go into.

First I thought I'd say a little more about *proprioception*. I understand some people still feel it's not clear. The basic thing is that you are directly aware of your body, of how your body is moving; whereas if you watch a tree moving, for instance, you are aware that that's quite independent of you. Proprioception makes you aware of your whole body as belonging to you, as part of you. You're aware of what is happening and how your intentions affect it, and so forth. And we can always get better at proprioception. People who are skilled, such as athletes or dancers, must have a very good proprioception of exactly how they are moving. They don't have to stop to think. They may have an intention in their thought as to what they want to do; but while they are actually doing it they don't stop to analyse exactly how it's going and compare that with what they intended.

That's the kind of thing that is involved in proprioception. But that awareness can break down. I read about somebody who had something happen to him, and then afterwards he felt that the right side of his body didn't belong to him – he was no longer aware of it as his own. The point is that we are immediately aware of the difference between a movement which originates by itself and one which we have thought about, without actually having to think 'this is what I'm aware of'.

I'm suggesting that this proprioception should be extended into thought, so that we are aware of thought as it participates. Thought's participation produces all sorts of things. And it affects perception – what you *think* affects what you perceive outside and how you feel inside.

Q: I wonder about that example you gave yesterday of the woman who had lost all proprioception and had to use her eyes to retrain herself. As we're sitting here, all of us are using proprioception or we wouldn't be able to stay in our chairs.

Bohm: Yes, that's a very good example. Suddenly she woke up without proprioception and she couldn't move her body in any controllable or orderly way. She couldn't sit up or do anything. She had to watch everything to see what was happening, and managed somehow to learn to get along that way.

It's very hard to explain, but as you're sitting in the chair you are aware of your body. You may not notice it, but there is an awareness of your body touching the chair and of the various little movements you have to make to correct for the fact that you are starting to fall, and so on. This is all part of proprioception. You're not really thinking about it or making decisions about it or making choices or anything like that. Rather, it's just working.

Now, we are asking whether proprioception could work similarly with thought – where you would become directly aware that your thought is affecting your perceptions. We have discussed how thought affects perceptions. You see or feel something produced by thought, but then the next thought comes along and says 'I'm only telling you the way it is'. Thought makes that claim, while it is actually affecting the way things are. That mistake is crucial. It's the same as not having proprioception in the body.

Q: I used to think that proprioception of thought is linear and that I had to follow my train of thought, which is sort of a contradiction. And so I realized that I had to be aware of my thought through sensation.

Bohm: The thought gives rise to sensation, yes. Even the impulse to think is a sensation. And then your thought gives rise to further sensations and images.

Q: If while I'm talking to you I become so fascinated with my talking that I lose the experience of the body, of sensation, then that would be thought to be functioning without what you're calling proprioception. But if I come back into my body and I talk to you, then there's some sense of these hands moving, the feel of this chair, the quality of the voice. Then it's a different process. Is that what you're suggesting?

Bohm: Yes, and all the different sensations which come from what you are saying.

Q: Are we speaking of a unified field of awareness, which includes thought but doesn't exclude the physical?

Bohm: Yes. But I'm saying that thought is part of the physical. Yesterday I made the point that thought is a more subtle form of the physical. Perhaps we should discuss that some more.

Thought is part of a material process. It goes on in the brain, the nervous system, and really the whole body and everything; it's all one system. Thought can be conveyed by material processes such as radio waves, television, writing – all kinds of ways. In talking, sound goes out and conveys thought. Within the body thought is conveyed by nervous signals; there is a code of some sort, which we don't know too well.

We're saying that thought is a material process; it has

147

reflexes that just go on by themselves. And if you have an insight or perception that this is true, then that will actually affect you. An insight or a perception of truth may deeply affect the material process, which includes all the reflexes. But if we merely have an intellectual or inferential knowledge of what is going on, then it doesn't touch this process deeply.

Q: When what you're calling an insight takes place, in effect a reorganization has taken place. And this isn't something I have or know about in my thinking, but simply that the functioning is then somewhat different.

Bohm: Yes, there has been a change. Let's suppose we use synapses in the brain as a kind of representation, although there is much more to it than that. You have all the nerves which connect through synapses. And they can make a set of synapses that produce a certain reflex which doesn't make sense, but just keeps going anyway. Just as thought acts and participates, so every perception acts and participates. Now by means of this perception of truth or insight, that perception acts. And it acts directly in the system and somehow makes a change so that the reflex becomes inoperative. Perhaps it starts to dissolve away a bit. You mustn't dissolve all the synapse connections away or else you wouldn't be able to do anything. It has to be done intelligently.

Have you ever seen something which seemed very attractive to you, and suddenly you had a perception of what it really was, and you said: 'It doesn't attract me anymore at all. I'm dead to it.' Do you see what I mean? There was a chemical sense inside of desire, of wanting something; and suddenly it stops. The chemistry is affected by the perception.

We discussed yesterday that matter may be infinitely subtle. Science doesn't know all about it, and probably never will. But matter is not just mechanical. Therefore, it could respond to that perception in very deep and subtle ways which may be beyond what science could even trace. So there can be a change. That's the notion: that the insight or perception will affect the whole thing. It not only affects the inferential understanding, but it also affects the chemical level and everything.

Q: What if we see it all as a unified process?

Bohm: But we won't even 'see' it, because when it works it's too fast for you to know what's happened – you get it in a flash. Later on you put it in words. Now, this question is crucial: when an insight is put into words, what is it that puts it into words? Is it thought or is it the insight? I want to suggest that the insight itself will be an insight into the words which express it properly. It's almost as though the words are coming out from a loudspeaker, rather than by somebody trying to get them out.

Q: What are bodily gestures in the context of what we are discussing?

Bohm: That's part of the expression, it's not the result of thought. Whatever is going on expresses itself through words, through gestures and in various other ways. The expression, whether verbal or not, is part of the perception or the insight; it is the action of the insight. And the expression is important, because the perception will not only change some of the – call it synapses or whatever – but it will also convey to thought the essential content of the insight. So thought can then proceed on a different basis, in a new direction. Therefore, it's important that it be expressed in words. But those words have to come from the insight. If, on the other hand, the words are just from memory, they may not be expressing it.

Q: Are you saying that when you have an insight into this creative process, it's in a mode that is not language – and that is a creative act? And it's another creative act of the brain to transform that into a language of words which we can communicate?

Bohm: Yes. But I think that it's all one act. The creative act simultaneously alters some of the reflexes and also produces the expression, in words or some other means, which will enable thought to take it up and move in a different way from there on.

Q: I wonder if a simple analogy would be the difference between memorizing a bunch of multiplication tables and understanding a formula. Once there is understanding of the relationship, then the overhead of remembering all the other data is gone and you can now relate to it.

Bohm: Yes. When you understand something, in some way it touches at a deeper level and then it will come out in words again.

The point is that we have the possibility of insight. Suppose we ask ourselves: 'Do we have it as an insight that thought is a material process, or that thought always participates in perception?' If we have that insight then that may remove some of the barriers to operating that way.

But our whole set of reflexes is against that. It says 'thought is not a material process'. Our first reflex is: 'Thought is far beyond matter, or separated from matter somehow. It has some spiritual truth or significance.' This notion has been conditioned into us as a reflex.

Now, however, we're saying thought is a material process and thought participates – which means the notion that thought is only telling you what things are is not really a serious option. If that comes as an insight, or if you get the insight that thought is not proprioceptive but requires proprioception, then that is going to begin to touch the synapses which hold those reflexes. The words will then also produce a change in thought, and thought will begin to stop getting in the way of seeing these things.

150

Our conditioning contains various barriers to proprioception, one of which is that thought implicitly says proprioception is not necessary. And if thought *were* only telling you the way things are, then proprioception would not be necessary because there would be nothing to perceive. Therefore, the notion that thought is only telling you the way things are is not a serious option; it's not a serious thing to consider. Is that clear? When you have that insight you are no longer taking seriously those things which previously loomed all-important. You're dead to them, whereas previously they moved you very much and had tremendous meaning. Now you say: 'They have no meaning. They're just mechanical stuff.'

Q: Apparently there are degrees of proprioception. Is this related to awareness as well as to non-awareness or non-mindfulness? And are there other people besides Krishnamurti who may have had a higher level of proprioception or mindfulness of what is taking place?

Bohm: That may all be, but we're liable to get into the domain of speculations which are carried into the system. We would put that into our system of thoughts and reflexes, and it would become a kind of knowledge which would get in the way. So there's a danger in this kind of imaginative speculation. The important point is actually to see for yourself the proprioception of thought, to see it in action.

I would like to discuss the *imagination* so that we could understand its role here, because it is very closely related to this question. 'Imagination' means 'making an image', 'seeing the image of something that is not there'; in other words, fantasy, fancy, and so on. But really there is no fundamental distinction between the processes of imagination and perception. We've said that the entire consciousness is actually created by a *process* which is being guided by information from the senses.

That process gives rise to our perception, and that process

is a kind of imagination. You could call that *primary* imagination.

Also, we can start to imagine things which are not there, things which are not indicated by perception. And that may be *creative* imagination. We can imagine forms of things that are unknown, which can then be brought into existence.

And we have another kind of imagination, which comes from the past, from the reflexes – the *reflexive* imagination, which could be called 'fancy' or 'fantasy'. This again could be useful, because we can imagine things and imagine ourselves going in certain ways or doing certain things, and solve problems that way. But it can be dangerous because this fantasy may slip over into apparent perception; it can participate in perception the way we said that thought does. When you're lost in fantasy, you seem to be almost perceiving the thing imagined. And you are not only apparently perceiving what you fantasize, you are apparently experiencing and perceiving the self that is doing it. In other words, it's all built out of thought. You can be an entirely different person in fantasy from what you would be outside, such as is portrayed in the book, *The Secret Life of Walter Mitty*.

Therefore, in fantasy you can create yourself and create a world. But then fantasy may start to merge with your perception of reality. Some people have suggested that when the infant's memory first starts to work it's mostly fantasy. According to the child psychologist Piaget, young children do have a lot of fantasy in thought. They may imagine that they are magically affecting things. And then they have to learn to distinguish certain 'fantasies' which are to be called 'reality', namely the ones that pass the tests for reality: those which stand up, which everybody sees, which resist being pushed, which are not affected by how you think about them, and so forth.

So the reality which you perceive is affected by your thought. Thought is working as a kind of imagination being infused into your perception. It becomes part of what you see. And that imagination is necessary. But if it gets held too strongly and resists evidence of incoherence, then it leads to all the problems we're talking about.

That's the general picture. You can see therefore that you have to watch the imagination carefully. It can be creative and it can be also very destructive, because the fantasy realm can merge with reality and create a resistance to seeing that it is fantasy. It will create reflexes that resist seeing it, because you create such beautiful fantasies that you don't want to give them up. They feel very good, the endorphins are produced and everything else. Hence, there is a movement – a reflex – to hold them and to resist thoughts which say that they are not right, or they are not the way it is. Thus you get illusion and all that.

I think that this notion of fantasy will help you to understand better how thought can enter into perception. And even when you don't think you are fantasizing it is still entering perception, because perception is all basically of the same nature as the process of imagination. If you think of the fact that perception is created from the brain in response to information, it follows inevitably that we can easily produce perceptions which are not right; and we have to correct them.

Q: What about the incoherence due to psychological addiction, but which includes chemical addiction – such as that of the alcoholic or the drug addict? This too can affect perception.

Bohm: Yes. But psychological addiction is always the most difficult one. For example, experiments have been done where animals were injected with some drug, maybe morphine, which made them chemically addicted. There were two groups – one was enabled to inject itself and the other was injected. Then the drug was withheld from both groups. The group that was injected went through a withdrawal process and was no longer addicted. The animals that were able to press the button to inject themselves got through the withdrawal process, but whenever they saw the button they pressed it again, even though it no longer gave them the drug. The point is that the memory of that pleasure produced a reflex to press the button. The button stirred up the whole system of memory.

Q: Are fantasy and imagination mostly based on memory and past experiences?

Bohm: I said that there are several kinds of imagination. There is the imagination based on memory, which is either remembering the past or projecting the future. In addition, there is a creative imagination which can project something new which you can then bring into existence – for example, a new idea to create something which was never there. In fact, a great many things we see here were the result of that.

And I'm saying that *perception* is a process similar to *imagination*. Now, this is the key thing. But we have no control over it. It just happens. It's going on and creates the whole impression of a world. That world includes not only what we sense – what we immediately perceive – but also the effect of the past. Thought is affecting our perception.

Q: In fantasy is there never creativity?

Bohm: In general no, because it's based on the past. I think there is a real distinction between creative imagination and fantasy. Fantasy may look very creative and feel very creative, but it may not be. You can even fantasize that you are being very creative. Anything can be fantasized; the power of fantasy is beyond limit. And it has its place – for instance, if you imagine arranging things in a room a different way that's fantasy but that may be useful.

Q: Is the perception of images in words, in itself, a physical sensory type of perception?

154

Bohm: It is part of the physical process, yes. It is very similar to the process which occurs when you actually see and hear, but it's coming partly from memory.

Q: Then it's an actual physical thing in the brain and the body, and it kind of all comes together?

Bohm: Yes.

Q: I see that part of the problem is that we have repressed words and images which are very quick. We're used to them and don't see that they're there. And when we think we are experiencing pure perception we need to be aware that the word and image are colouring that perception to create pleasure. What is the insight that can break the addiction to pleasure?

Bohm: Let's look at it first for a while. In fantasy you can create pleasure, pain, fear, anything, because you are producing from memory an experience similar to what might be produced if it weren't memory. If you are sensitive you always can tell there is a difference, but the fantasy may captivate you so far that you're not sensitive to the difference. In fact, you may not want to know the difference, because it has created a reflex, saying: 'This is so nice I don't want to know any more. I don't want to know about it. I don't want evidence that it may not be so.' Everybody is familiar with that experience.

But you can see that it's basically coming from memory, from thought. By words you can create fantasies. For example, that's what advertising is doing all the time. The combination of words and images creates fantasy. The purpose is to create the expectation or the sense of the pleasure you will get, or the advantages you will get out of the product they are selling. It's aimed to get you to fantasize something about that product. A great deal of work is required to produce those advertisements. They think it out very thoroughly and the images have to be carefully chosen and connected with the words. You can see how this process is going on all around. The advertisers didn't invent it. They're only taking advantage of something that's been going on for ages.

Now you ask 'what about an insight or perception?'. Well, we can't make that to order. But I'm suggesting that we can have an insight that thought and fantasy can produce a sense of 'reality'.

Q: I feel I have that insight. But because of the pleasure that one gets from it – because there's that connection in the brain or whatever, that mechanism by which these fantasies create pleasure or create pain – it seems as though one somehow needs to break that connection.

Bohm: Yes, you need a further insight into why the mind is escaping the consequences of the first insight. Although we have an insight at the level of inference, these reflexes are still working.

So one thing to do is just to get more familiar with it by watching it, by using the words which produce the pleasure in the same way that we've talked about using the words to call up anger or fear, and follow it through. I think if you stay with it and build up that pleasure from those words, you will eventually get the sense that it is mechanical, that it's just something going on in the body. It hasn't a great significance.

Q: I see it slightly differently. Let's say I have this insight. Somehow the reflex comes up, the synapse connection is there, but it doesn't have the hold. It's like, 'well, so it's going to do its thing, but I don't believe in it in the same way'.

Bohm: That weakens it. But you can, if you wish, sort of do this exercise of really making the reflex work now that it has been weakened. Until it had been weakened you couldn't do this. As long as you believed in the reflex, the idea of doing this would have been impossible. You could now say 'I don't believe in it anymore and therefore I can try to make the reflex work', and become very much more clear that it is a reflex.

Q: And if one does what you're suggesting would that speed up the process of getting rid of the synapse?

Bohm: It might, yes. It might do something, and then at some stage you would have an insight that the whole thing has no meaning – it's just simply a mechanical process.

Q: But at that point, the insight isn't something which is happening about the words anymore. Rather, it's some direct perception of the crossover between fantasizing and perceiving, *in* the process of that happening.

Bohm: Yes, you get a direct sense of that; and that begins to remove those reflexes which were telling you that it's the other way around. The thing which is confusing us is that we still have a lot of reflexes telling us it's not that way at all.

Q: I don't know whether it's a problem, but what about the reflex of questioning all the reflexes?

Bohm: You have to question these reflexes because you've had an insight that there is a vast number of reflexes and there is no reason why they should be intelligent. That's the insight.

Q: I think of the reflex as a button. When the button is being

157

pushed, can there be an insight into its action while it's happening, rather than thinking about it later?

Bohm: Yes, or even before it happens, because you have seen through this so thoroughly that you have no wish to press the button.

Q: But the real proof of the insight, if we're going to call it that, is that the thing just doesn't happen.

Bohm: Yes, but we have to test the insight, because we can always fantasize that we've had it. We can test the insight by seeing whether it stands up reasonably and logically, whether we are actually able to do it, and so on. You have to watch it all the time, because it's very easy to have a fantasy of an insight and say that you've had an insight.

Q: We have to be careful when using the word 'insight', and be sensitive to what insight is. It's not that *I* am making the insight, but it's that the insight happens.

Bohm: Or else to be sensitive to something that can be mistaken for insight.

Q: Thought can deceive itself. It can fabricate the impression of an insight, but that has nothing to do with insight.

Bohm: Yes, that's the reflexive imagination. You can get imagination which comes from the memory and which is a reflex; so it's not really relevant to this. But when you see something new you could even say that the insight is almost a kind of creative imagination, but one which actually acts directly in the material process.

The nervous structure, synapses and so on are so infinitely

complex that the memory could never handle it all. The memory could never know all that, you could never know it all. But the insight is able to meet that as it actually is, at the moment – this is the crucial thing – without *time*. If it takes time it won't meet it.

Q: In a way I think you could almost say that no one could ever 'have' an insight – that within a particular organism something might occur, and after the fact someone might say that that was an insight. But whether you imagined it or something actually happened, it would never be anything you had, but just that there might be a different organization within the organism.

Bohm: Yes. That insight took place and there was a change in the organism. The insight is probably from immense depths of subtlety – perhaps even beyond the organism for all we know. Wherever it comes from, the important point is that it works directly at the physical chemical level of the organism, along with everything else. So it really affects you through and through.

Q: Is insight available to all of us? And does it take an emotional opening for it to come in?

Bohm: We don't know where it comes from. I'm suggesting that it is available to all of us. But the reflex of thought is continually resisting and defending against it, because the insight may be seen as a threat to the structure which you want to hold.

Q: Insight affects the conditioning; it may even be that not a lot of it survives – that a lot of the conditioning dies, it dissolves.

Bohm: It's a threat to the conditioning, yes. But the conditioning is, in fact, not all that important. However, the conditioning contains a reflex which informs you that the conditioning is very important.

Now, I wonder if we shouldn't go into the question of the *self-image*. We've already sort of touched on it by thinking of the imagination and fantasy giving a sense of a self that could be very different from your usual sense. And you really feel it, you experience it. Or you can be watching television or a play or a movie and getting lost in the characters and feel that that character actually is you. In fact, you're experiencing the character through yourself, because the television image is nothing but a lot of dots of light on the screen. All the things you see in there are really yourself.

And that's how you perceive everything. Clearly, there is a kind of imagination involved in looking at the television image. If you were to look at it carefully you would see nothing but flashing lights. But you see people, trees, characters; you see emotional conflicts and danger; you see anger, fear, pleasure. But it's all yourself. It's all the imagination being infused into the picture on the screen – just as it gets infused into perception. So when you're looking at the television set, what you experience must come from something like the imagination. Where else could it come from?

It becomes more and more clear how thought enters into perception. Thought, though, doesn't know it's doing it. In fact, most of the time you don't need to know. However, when there is incoherence you do need to know. This is the point: if there is a resistance to knowing it when you need to know, if there are reflexes that resist knowing, then there is trouble.

You can't keep track of all that – every time you watch the television set, thinking 'well, this is really me, projecting into the television screen'. It's like the rainbow. I see a rainbow out there; but according to physics, actually there are drops of rain falling and light refracting off of them. The same sort of thing happens when you're looking at the television. There are spots of light, and you see all sorts of things happening; but it's the same nature as the rainbow. It's closer to the actuality to say that there is a process going on in the television set – a complex process with the light, with your nerves, with everything. You can't get hold of it all. It's a representation; that drama is representing something in many, many levels. And what you see and experience is that representation.

I'm trying to make it more clear how this thing is actually a very common experience and not so hard. We are infusing our imagination, our past, our knowledge into what we see – not 'we' are doing it, but it's doing it itself. And that isn't necessarily bad. It may be very necessary in many contexts. However, when we fail to see that this is happening then we are in danger, especially if there is resistance to seeing it. And we are conditioned to resist seeing that this is happening. That's really where the self-deception arises.

Now, it's around the self-image that the problem is most difficult. We've got a kind of self-image that is almost like a television programme going on inside; its going on in the nerves, and so forth. And this image has several parts. One part seems to be 'somebody' inside at whom you are looking. Another part seems to be 'somebody' who is looking. We have different words for these. The word 'I' stands for the subject, the one who sees, who acts, who does, who determines everything, who has *will*. 'Will' is the same as 'determine' and 'intention'. 'I am determined' means strong will. 'I' is the active agent: I will, I determine, I see, I choose, I think. And also there is 'me' to whom it's all done. 'Me' is the object, everything happens to me. Then, the basic concept, the 'self', is what unites those two. *I* and *me* are two sides of *myself*. So there are me, myself and I. That's a concept of the self.

We've discussed this many times, that the word 'I' by itself means almost the same as God. It's the ultimate source of everything. In the story of Moses who came to the burning bush in the desert and asked the voice what was its name, the voice said that His name was 'I Am That I Am'. 'I Am' was His first name and 'I Am' was His second name. Later the voice said again that 'I Am' was his name; when Moses asked 'who shall I say sent me?' the voice said 'You shall say that "I am" sent you'. Evidently 'I Am' was considered to be the name of God, which was very sacred, not supposed to be repeated, and so on.

That's a kind of perception – that the phrase 'I am' by itself represents the pure subject, the pure source, the one, the source of everything; and that 'me' represents the object. But we identify or equate 'I am' with 'me', saying 'I am this, I am that, I am what I am, I am all the things attributed to *me*'. However, there comes a problem in equating 'I am' with 'me', because 'me' is always limited; 'little you', they say, 'who are you to think you are great, the great "I Am"?'. Whereas 'I am', without adding anything more, does not have any implicit limitation.

The essential point is that the 'me' is always limited, but we feel that 'me' is the same as 'I am', as 'I'. Now, this creates a conflict. People want to say: 'I'm the greatest. I'm the best. I'm the most wonderful.' We have this great, bright and shining image. And then the world comes along and says 'You're nothing. You're just fooling yourself. You're nobody.' It deflates that image, which becomes a shock and creates a great pain – the fantasy of pleasure can equally turn into the fantasy of pain and fear and horror. In a fantasy you can really get into all that.

But it's very hard to keep the thought of 'I' and 'me' orderly – to make sense of it, to make it coherent. People don't know how to resolve this contradiction between 'I am' and 'me'. People say: 'You should not treat me as an object. I don't like it. I'm insulted, hurt.' And society says: 'Who do you think you are that you should be different from everybody else and not be treated as an object? You think that you shouldn't be limited.' Yet 'me', by definition, is an object.

The little child may feel that there is no limit, that he's everything. He forms that thought, that reflex, that fantasy. Whether it reflects anything real or not we don't know. What is important is that it sets up a reflex, saying 'that's *me*'. He would hardly form an identity without that. He also depends

on other people to tell him what he is and who he is. However the great, bright and shining being he sees from within
is not always seen from without. Other people don't back
that up. They may treat him as God when he's a very young
child, but then a time suddenly appears when they don't.

So you have this tremendous conflict. You have what Freud
called the narcissistic image. There's the Greek legend of
Narcissus, who saw a beautiful man in the water and didn't
realize it was his own image. He fell in love with it. But he
could never get to that image, and he pined away and died.
The irony was he already had that for which he was longing,
he already *was* that for which he was longing. However, he
didn't believe it or wouldn't accept it. He said 'that's somebody else, whom I need'.

The point is: when we produce this self-image in fantasy
it then becomes the thing longed for. And we say 'there it is
far away from me, and I've got to reach it'. But this is another
fantasy, another image. And it creates the sense 'I need to
have that'.

The sense of necessity gives the greatest force and power
there is in human affairs. You can't resolve that. And the
child never really learns – not in our current society, nor
probably in any society of which we know – to get free of
this image, to get free of being bound to this image.

Therefore, when the image is punctured it hurts. The fantasy of this great, glorious, shining being is then turned into
a fantasy of somebody who is despised and looked down
upon and limited – who is nothing much, and all that sort
of thing – which creates pain. And that creates the need to
have other people tell me how great I am and it creates the
sense 'I need to get proof of how great I am by what I do or
by what I own', and that sort of thing.

This is very powerful. Human affairs are very powerfully
dominated by all that. And a megalomaniac would say 'I
must govern the world in order to show what I am', as did
Alexander the Great. It was reputed that neither he nor his
mother ever got along with his father. He identified with
his mother, and somehow they came to hate his father. Prob-

ably he felt a strong necessity to show his father how great he was, so to do that he conquered the world. And then when he had done that, he said that he was very sad because he had no more worlds to conquer. In other words, he had to keep on conquering the world, he never could stop, because he had to feed that image all the time.

Q: But the philosopher Diogenes beat him down. He was living in nature, enjoying the sunshine, and Alexander the Great came and stood in front of him and cast a shadow. The philosopher said to him: 'Could you please get away? You are blocking something you can't give me – the sunshine.' The wisdom of the philosopher beat down his image.

Bohm: Well, I suppose Alexander probably always suspected that it wasn't quite true. I mean, he wasn't stupid; he was really very intelligent. But he was caught in this image. And he had tremendous power because of it. People would do anything for him because he had such power. You can see how this whole thing works. Everybody has this same image, which has been beaten down. However, if the soldiers saw Alexander the Great with a bright glorious shining image, they could identify with it; they would feel, 'I'm that way too'. So they would do anything for him. Whatever he said for them to do, they did. And therefore they became very powerful.

You can see the power of all this imagination and fantasy. Throughout all the world that sort of thing has produced effects like that. There was Hitler, and there have been all sorts of other people. And we haven't resolved this question.

The point is now that this self-image contains two parts. At first that seems reasonable, because even physically there is 'I' who is looking and 'I' at whom the looking is done – 'I' who is the subject and 'I' who am the object. I say: 'Here is my body. I am looking at it.' The body is the object of the looking. But I am also the subject – 'I' who am looking. It seems that I am looking at myself – a reflexive act. It makes sense, right? I wash myself, I shave myself, I do all sorts of things like that.

And then when we form the image inside it seems that there is 'I' who is the subject, looking at 'me' who is the object. Down in the chest area somewhere perhaps is the object, and up in the head is somebody looking. That can be arranged by fantasy quite easily – we've discussed how thought enters perception: once thought says that that's the way it is, then we perceive it that way.

But now if that 'thing' which is perceived in that way were actually there, it would be extremely important and precious, wouldn't it? It would be this great, glorious shining God – or at least it ought to be. It would be the centre of existence and everything. For the little child it is. And in fact, it never goes away for anybody. So that which is inside here has tremendous importance and necessity. It's not merely the chemistry, but the chemistry is given extremely high value by the importance and necessity attached to the meaning. They go together, because there are enormous chemical effects going on – neurophysiological effects of such a great shining image, which is perceived as reality, and also tremendous meaning which holds it. Therefore, when all that doesn't work properly it really disorganizes the system.

Thus this self-image becomes central. And everything becomes arranged to feed and sustain it in as good a way as possible. We try to arrange thoughts that way. We try to get people to support it. We try to produce situations, such as acquiring wealth – people will make a lot of money to show that they are really very great people. They make far more money than they need for whatever they want to do. They keep on making money. And if the mere making of money isn't enough, then they buy all sorts of things – far more than they need – to show that they are great people.

Why do people do this? It's accepted, it's taken for granted that they will do it. But we need to look into this. Why? What's behind it? You can see that there is a process going on here which involves the whole system. And people will reinforce each other in all of it, because people get their identity from one another – everybody says 'you are this, you are that, you are the other'. Or else you get your identity by what you do, or by thinking of where you came from, or what your ancestors were, and all that. So you get a sense of identity built up out of thought, which says 'that's terribly important'. You have to prove that you're there.

But this structure actually has no basis whatsoever except thought, which is a very flimsy base. And since that structure apparently is all-important, it would be very important to prove that it is solidly grounded. Otherwise it will be rather alarming to see this all-important structure with no ground.

Q: I've asked myself who I am, and realized that I am several images at once – each of my children has a different image of me, as do my husband, friends and anyone else. But I feel I'm not those images, I'm something else. Even that 'something else' comes into question, as what I think I am changes from one day to the next. I put a question about my body, and asked whether I would be less of who I think I am if I had one arm less, or whatever, than I now have. So I decided I am not my body. There is something else, but I can't explain what it is.

Bohm: Well, that's the problem: how are we going to find what we are? You can't exist without your body, but usually people don't take it all that seriously. Their identity is what they can do or what they have or what their relations are; that's usually taken as more important. People will allow their bodies to degenerate in favour of that. Other people may regard their bodies as all-important. It can vary. You can put your identity into almost anything – into your country, or into your bank account or into your achievements – into anything.

But the whole thing doesn't seem to have any ground. Now, if this self were what it's apparently supposed to be, then it would be very important to get a real solid ground for it. And that's why we feel the urge to search for this identity. Yet people are not really that sure about their identity. The question is: do we need an identity? Clearly in some limited sense we do need to know who we are – we have identity cards, we have memories and needs and certain relationships, and all the rest. We keep that all straight. But is that identity the supremely important thing that it seems to be?

Q: Does the identity depend on the system you were talking about?

Bohm: I'm saying that the system gives you the identity. Without the system you would have no identity. The whole system of thought spread over the world is what gives you your identity, your place in the world and so forth. If there were no system, how could you sustain that identity? The identity could only exist socially and culturally. Although we may try to identify ourselves with God, or something like that, there again it's the culture which gave you the thought allowing you to do that. That's what we have to keep in mind.

There was an ancient view: '*I don't know what I am. What I am is unknown, but constantly revealing itself.*' This is another view of what you are. Let's look at it for a moment. 'I' am unknown. If there is something which is infinite – the universe, or something beyond the universe – I am somehow grounded in that. Maybe the whole physical being, and probably even matter, is infinite in its subtlety. And there may be something beyond. Therefore, whatever I am, *that* must be the source of it. *That* is unknown – but it reveals itself. We don't need the notion of an identity, of an all-important identity on to which we are going to hold, because that gets in the way of the need to change our reflexes. Once we identify with something, our reflexes *are* that way – it's very important, 'necessary'. And we will want to preserve that identity even though it may involve ideas that are false.

167

Q: Are you saying that it's very important for us to preserve the particular kind of chemistry that we're used to?

Bohm: That's what it amounts to, implicitly – that identity will give us a certain chemistry. And also we *feel* that we want to preserve that. The whole body gets used to it. The body itself can get used to a certain chemistry, and demands that that chemistry be preserved. So thought will try to do that. But in addition, thought has put it that there is, more abstractly, an identity that has to be preserved – which is absolutely *necessary*.

Q: I'll just see if I can say it in my own words. The identity lies in abstractions, which are images; and each one of those images is a continuum, has a chemistry. And that chemistry in some sense has a *reality* to it, and is all movement?

Bohm: Yes, it's all movement. It includes chemistry and possibly some material reality beyond chemistry – the physics, the electricity, and beyond that.

Q: Say I find this out from someplace; and *I*, in my abstractions, would like to change. But I don't have any notion that it's not the images that have to change – it's the chemistry that has to change.

Bohm: The whole thing has to change. We may change the images, but the chemistry doesn't change that way. The whole thing has to change: we need an insight into the whole.

Q: Could the fixedness of the chemistry be the cause of disease?

Bohm: The fixedness of the chemistry and the fixedness of

168

the ideas around it are inseparable, because if your ideas about the chemistry say that it is absolutely necessary to maintain it, then that helps fix the chemistry. You can't say that the chemistry is fixed independently of the ideas that the system as a whole is carrying about the chemistry.

Q: Is the need to label things and people and to put them into little boxes part of this holding on to images?

Bohm: That's part of the image – that we put people into boxes, as you say. And they may actually have several different boxes; there's an expression about wearing several different hats – such as when you're at work you have one hat and when you're at home you have another one.

So the whole process is not coherent. When you begin to look at it, you see that it doesn't hold together. That's the incoherence of the image. And if you really see it – if you really don't believe it anymore – then you have to say that making the image all-important is not a serious option.

It may be that it's still going to operate, it still has a large amount of chemistry that we haven't got at, and so on. But a very crucial step right here is the insight that this whole process actually has no meaning. It has no ground. It's truly the most ephemeral sort of thing. There's nothing more ephemeral than thoughts; and yet thoughts can hold themselves by saying 'I must remain this way forever, with absolute necessity'. The point is to have the notion of a *creative* being, rather than of an *identified* being.

Q: As ephemeral as thought may be, is thought not in fact in the brain cells themselves?

Bohm: It's in the brain cells, but as an ephemeral movement – it comes and goes, it mixes up with the chemistry and the electrical currents, and all that.

169

Q: If the identity movement is strong it can be a block to the creative energy.

Bohm: Yes, it certainly blocks it. The identity movement may be the major block. We've been following the blocks all along, and now this may be very close to the source of the major block – the attempt to hold this identity, which is part of the reflex system.

Q: I don't think people have taken the danger of identification seriously so far. At this moment, as you're making it clear, it seems that there is a real danger in having an identity. The ephemeral movement of identity can block the energy; it can be a strong addiction, because it gets close to the power of necessity.

Bohm: Yes, it all ties up. We could look at that. The identity has a certain limited significance. It's not that we are going to dispose of it, but it has no fundamental deep eternal significance.

There is eternal flow and movement that is creative. But this creativity can get caught up in a certain process, which appears to be mechanical. The process isn't really mechanical, because it can always change with new insight. If it were a machine it could never change. I'm saying it isn't fully deeply a machine, but it can behave something like a machine. So we can represent this process as mechanical, but only up to a point.

We'll leave it at that for now and take our break.

Bohm: We've been discussing this self-image – the self as observer and the self as observed. They seem to be separate because they have been imaged that way. The image produces the perception of that separation.

Perhaps, if you want, we'll talk about it for a little while. We said that clearly the human being actually is *there* in some sense – he is actual. The question is: does the human being exist with a permanent identity? And, if there is one, what would it be? We said that this notion of identity doesn't seem to be very coherent. The whole basis is very ephemeral, insubstantial in thought.

Then there was the suggestion of another way of looking at the human being. The ground of any person is really unknown. It might be in the whole totality of whatever is – of all matter, even beyond matter. We ourselves are matter which has come together from all over the world. The carbon in us has probably come from carbon dioxide, which has been diffusing over the entire atmosphere. It may have been somewhere on the other side of the world and it got into plants and into animals, and so forth, and then got into us. Likewise with the oxygen and water, and so on. So materially our ground is really in the whole universe. Thus, you could then follow it through scientifically and say that it came from the earth, and that the earth was formed from hot gas which came from stars, or whatever, and those came from interplanetary dust – on and on, back to the Big Bang and even beyond. Therefore, we could say all of that has conspired to produce *us* – the material structures that we are. Thus, we would have to say that in some sense this matter is *actual*.

But our thoughts about it are not actual. They are representations, they contain forms. The thought about the table contains a form. But the table doesn't actually end the way we see it – at the atomic level it would sort of shade out a bit. And in modern physics, one of the things they say is that empty space is full of energy, a vast amount of energy. Each wave in empty space has a certain minimum energy, even when it's empty, and if you add up all the waves it would be infinite. But if you add up waves down to a certain length called the Planck length (ten to the minus thirty-three centimetres – a very short distance – beyond which we might expect the present law of physics not to hold) the total in a cubic centimetre would be more than the energy of all the matter in the universe. The idea, then, is that space is mostly

171

full, and that matter is a small ripple on it. You can make a very strong case for that according to modern physics.

Similarly, we could say that whatever is behind the mind – the consciousness, or whatever you want to call it – is a vast stream; and on the surface are ripples which are thought. This seems to be an analogy. Even when we talk of things being 'here', they are really small ripples on some vast energy which is circulating. The only reason that this energy doesn't show up is because matter and light go right through it without deflecting. What we experience is empty space. But it may also be regarded as the fullness of space, which is the ground of all existence. Matter is, then, a small variation on this ground.

We now, however, begin to think of the forms in thought, by which we try to represent matter. Those forms are much more abstract than matter. We can elaborate those forms in all sorts of ways – make very realistic looking pictures, and so forth – but they are not the material things themselves. Like maps, those forms may serve as guides and lead to coherent action, if they are correct representations. Otherwise they lead to incoherence and all the problems that come from that.

That's the general picture. The things which we actually see are there in some sense; and we are going to discover in our relation with them that we will be coherent if there is correct thought. But the ground of the thing is much, much deeper. At the very least it's in the material structure, which is far more solid than the thought about it. And then beyond the material structure is another structure, which may be even infinitely more solid than that, or far more substantial than that.

Now, maybe mind is another 'side' of that same thing – that which we call energy on one side is mind on the other side. That is, energy is pervaded with a kind of intelligence, out of which perhaps insight comes, or deeper perceptions of truth. That's the suggestion.

Then what about ourselves? We say that our ground is in all that. But we have all sorts of representations of ourselves which are really rather superficial. And we try to identify with them. But then once we do that, we have this quality of thought which infuses it into perception. We apparently perceive the thing we are representing – it seems to be there. It's like the rainbow; we see a rainbow, but what we have is drops of rain and light – a process. Similarly, what we 'see' is a self; but what we actually have is a whole lot of thoughts going on in consciousness. Against the backdrop of consciousness we are projecting a self, rather than a rainbow. If you walk toward the rainbow you will never get there. The image of the table is produced in the same way, but if you walk toward the table you will get there and touch it.

I'm suggesting that if you try to touch the self, it will be the same difficulty as trying to touch the rainbow. We have a representation of the self, which is really arising in a process. We don't know this process very well; but the attempt to treat the self as an object is just not going to mean anything. So instead, suppose we say that this self is *unknown*. Its origin, its ground is *unknown*. And it is constantly revealing itself, through each person or through nature or through various other ways.

Q: The self is revealed?

Bohm: Whatever you mean by 'yourself'. The basic meaning of the word 'self', according to the dictionary, is the 'quintessence' – the essence of the essence. The fifth essence, it was called. There were four essences in ancient times and then they added a fifth one, which was the essence of the whole thing. The idea is that the thing 'itself' means the very essence of it. Thus what you mean by the 'self' is your very essence. You say 'I' and 'me', and 'myself' – 'self' being the essence from which the 'I' and me' have their ground. But that use of language will give rise to representations, which we are liable to mistake for actuality.

That's all I'm saying: whatever the self is, its essence is unknown but constantly revealing itself.

One point is to clear up the thought that we are something limited and known. I'm saying we cannot be that which

173

is limited and known. Nothing can be what is limited and known; that can at best be an abstraction or a representation. This actuality cannot be that.

Q: Would it help to look at this in terms of orientation difference? In one sense, what we're talking about is 'I' am learned. All the memory, the sense of identification of self at that level, is learned. A different orientation might be '*I* am learning'.

Bohm: If you are learning, yes. However, if you're learning you can't *know* – that you are learning implies the unknown. We could say that the unknown is therefore revealing itself in what you are learning. But there is always the unknown. In other words, we are not going to exhaust the unknown – we've said that even in physics there is this picture of the almost infinite energy in empty space. So the suggestion is that there is a vast unknown. It is revealing itself. We are learning, if you like; and even if we're not learning it is revealing itself.

That's the general notion. That's the *creative* view of being, rather than the idea of an *identity* of being.

Q: What is revealing itself?

Bohm: The unknown. The unknown ground of all that is. It reveals itself in many ways. That is a creative view, a creative notion of being. That's what we are suggesting, rather than a notion of identity – which is limited and repetitive, and so on.

We don't *know*. And if you once say 'I am this forever', then it sort of blocks things. You could always ask 'how do you know that's what you are?'. You may have been that way, but there is no proof that whatever has been will always be.

Q: If I hold up my hand I could say this is the unknown

revealing itself. If I look at your cup I can look at that as the unknown revealing itself.

Bohm: Yes, anything. The unknown may reveal itself in a similar way to what it was before. Many things just keep on revealing themselves in a certain similar way, though underneath it is eternal flux but producing a similar form which we are representing in our thought. Now, our thought is adequate for representing those forms, and it may hint at what's beneath, but it really cannot get hold of that.

Q: If I do something, such as make a painting, is that also the unknown revealing itself?

Bohm: It can be, or it could be from your memory. However, even the basic actuality of memory is the unknown. We have to say that everything we know is a form, which we sort of project onto the background of consciousness – as we do with the rainbow. It can be projected correctly or incorrectly; it's not that every form is as good as every other.

Many, many forms could be projected. We could have different cultures and different views of life, and all, which have different degrees of coherence. The important point is that the overall view is in the culture, and we have to ask how coherent it is. You can see that this thing is done not only individually, but even more so collectively. By sharing our thought and consciousness we are projecting forms into everything. We'll discuss that this afternoon in connection with dialogue.

Q: When you say culture is coherent or incoherent, are you saying that the representation, the abstraction, will either be coherent or incoherent? But the substance itself – the frame and the canvas of the painting, as it were – is always coherent.

Bohm: Yes, the material structure is always coherent, though it may not be what we think it is.

Q: Then incoherence can only lie in representations?

Bohm: In the forms of representations. And in the actions to which those forms lead.

Q: Is there nothing that's limited and known, except through looking at it wrongly?

Bohm: Thought always provides limits which have relative validity.

I'm suggesting that you have two possibilities. One is to say that everything is limited, and knowledge could 'get' it all. And the other is to say that knowledge cannot get it all. People are trying to find out what the ultimate knowledge is. Scientists thought they had it in the nineteenth century. And then they said 'no, it's not so'. Today there is no sign that we have the final theory yet, although people are talking about the 'theory of everything', which they hope to get. But you could say, first of all, that any knowledge we've ever had has been limited. Now that doesn't prove anything, but it makes one question.

Suppose even that physicists had finally found the theory of everything – the ultimate, final particles, which we'll call the 'ultimons'. And then it would just go on century after century. They would calculate in terms of the ultimons and everything would work out. But there would still be no proof that maybe in the next minute or next hour or day or century they wouldn't discover a limit to it all, and it wouldn't work.

In other words, there is no way to *know* that you've got it. So it's a poor strategy to assume it, because if you assume that you have the ultimate then you won't look for anything else, and therefore it will tend to trap you. You have no way of knowing that you have the ultimate. You may say something like 'God told me', but then people could say 'how do you know that?'. You can't ever get absolute assurance that you have ultimate knowledge, no matter how convinced you are of it. The best you can say is 'as far as I can see, that's the way it is'.

Q: Then the search for the ultimate in terms of knowledge might be a mistake in itself.

Bohm: Yes, it may be a very serious mistake – part of the flaw in the system we're talking about. We have to be open. You can see how important it is. If ultimate knowledge were possible about the atom it would imply that it might be possible about our identity, because we're made of atoms. Many scientists are working on that assumption – saying that we will have it all, that artificial intelligence will reproduce everything, and so forth. But I'm saying I think that that is an incoherent procedure.

Q: How would you differentiate between the search for ultimate knowledge and the search for something ultimate beyond knowledge?

Bohm: You can't search for it, because the very word 'search' implies trying to get hold of it. I think we have to say only that, as far as thought is concerned, we need to leave open the possibility that something beyond knowledge is possible, and indeed very plausible. First of all, we've said that there is a great deal of evidence that knowledge cannot be complete. And second, there has to be something beyond; but we have no proof. Then we ask 'is it possible to somehow come in contact with *that* in some other way?'. Maybe it would be possible and maybe not.

Q: Is the moving force the same for the search for ultimate knowledge and the beyond?

Bohm: I wouldn't think so. I think the search for ultimate knowledge would have to be a search for security. But we have to say that what is beyond – which is the unknown – cannot meaningfully be sought. If you would *really* see that, it may be that it would give security. But at least the way we picture it, the unknown doesn't look very secure.

Q: The way we picture it from this viewpoint.

Bohm: Yes. Maybe when you *are* that, then it may be secure.

Q: Are you suggesting knowledge isn't the barometer of knowing?

Bohm: We know that already, because knowledge is always subject to test for incoherence, which must get beyond knowing. You cannot know all the tests for incoherence.

Q: Then there is some other sensitivity in knowing, other than knowing being knowledge-based?

Bohm: Yes, knowing is a process based on the unknown.

Q: I wonder if we could look at the relationship between this ultimate self-image and the search for the ultimate knowing, and how that relates to what we were talking about before – the word creating the sensation, and so forth?

Bohm: If you assume, as the culture generally does, that there is an ultimate knowledge, then that will be perceived as something which is there as a possibility. Therefore your intentions, your impulse, your motivation will be toward it, because if there is such ultimate knowledge it would be the right thing to try to get it. Now, if there isn't, you will say: 'That's dead to me. I have no interest in that.'

Q: Universal 'truths' or 'ideas' seem to run across all countries and cultures – for instance, the Ten Commandments or the Golden Rule. Is that like a reflection, or is that just a self-image that's projected by all people on the planet?

Bohm: There may have been an insight that people have to be related in a certain way in order for society to work and for anything to have any meaning – an insight that you can't treat people totally immorally; that if you do so it will all come back to you, it won't work, it's incoherent.

Q: Would that be a projected self-image?

Bohm: No, I think the original insight was beyond that, but then thought takes hold of it and turns it into the system and projects the self-image. In other words, everything can be turned into this mill.

Q: Can we stay open-ended, without having expectations of acquiring knowledge or results, and let things flow and just 'let it be'?

Bohm: Well, that's a question we're raising. The only answer would be whether we do it or don't. We can't really answer this from knowledge. If it is unknown and it can't be answered from knowledge, it seems to call for something else, which we've been calling 'perception of truth' or 'insight'. And we have been going into various kinds of thoughts, looking at thoughts which are getting in the way of this and which are part of our culture.

Perhaps we all are having some insight into this at some level, that it has some effect. But it will require a lot of work

179

to get actually into all the chemistry which holds the old way.

That's the point I would like to make. Now, if you don't want to call it 'insight' you could call it 'perception of truth'. And we could raise the question of what is *truth*. Our culture has similarly produced a lot of confusion around that, which makes it hard to get into it.

One theory of truth is that true ideas correspond to reality, such as the true idea of the table would correspond to the reality of the table. But we've just seen that this can't be because every idea is a representation – an abstraction which leaves out most of the reality. It's hard to know what it corresponds to. For example, if a map is a correct map, does it correspond to anything in the country? On the map are lines and dots representing cities, roads, rivers and boundaries. Those lines on the map are abstractions. They are not actually lines anyway – if you look at them carefully you can see they are little dots, printed dots of ink, all strung near each other. And, similarly, the lines between the countries don't exist either. They've been imagined by people. A fence or wall may eventually be put up, but it was put up by people who thought there was a line there. Thus there is a correspondence between one abstraction and another, which guides you. But it's a correspondence of form, certain abstract forms, but not to reality – the reality itself escapes you. Every one of those things which corresponds in that way doesn't stand by itself as reality.

There may be a correspondence of that kind, which is part of a correct idea. And a correct idea will not only lead to that kind of correspondence, but also to coherent action. But I would like to say that truth is something more. An idea may be correct or incorrect or somewhere in between; but truth is something deeper. We should reserve the word 'truth' for something much deeper.

The root of the word 'true' in English means 'straight', 'honest' and 'faithful' – like 'a true line'. And in Latin, the word *verus* is a root word which means 'that which is'. So you could say that a rough idea of the meaning of the word 'truth' would be 'straight, honest and faithful to *that which is*'. But there will be no truth unless the mind is straight, honest and faithful; unless it doesn't engage in self-deception; unless the chemistry allows it. For truth to arise there must be a certain situation in the brain.

Q: In the Greek language the word for truth is *alethia*, which means 'out of lethargy', 'out of sleep'.

Bohm: 'Out of sleep', yes. You have to be awake, alert for truth. In other words, it requires what we may call a certain 'state of mind'; really, a state of the material system as well. What generally happens when the whole system is too jangled is that it is filled with all sorts of chemical effects of this incoherent thought, which interfere with perception and put you to sleep, and so forth. You could say the brain is filled with what I call 'electrochemical smog'. And when that is present we don't have truth.

I think the idea that there is an abstract truth – somewhere, somehow, sitting there waiting for us get hold of it – is again the same as the idea of the ultimate knowledge. Truth is something more vital. It has to be that sort of movement which doesn't deceive itself. And then it has to fit, cohere with 'that which is'. Truth is a perception, and is simultaneously an action. The action of truth would clear up the electrochemical smog. It clears up the smog, as it were, so that you see more clearly. And also the system isn't being poisoned, and whatnot. So that's part of truth. Truth is not merely information *about* 'what is'. But rather truth is a key factor *in* 'what is'.

Q: How does truth relate to the unknown self revealing itself?

Bohm: The source of truth must be like the source of insight – beyond what thought can grasp. And truth comes and touches the physical chemical state of the brain, as well as producing the words which communicate it to thought.

Truth is not just floating out there abstractly, but truth actually *is*. That is to say, truth is a factor in actuality. Truth *meets* 'that which is'; it touches 'that which is' in a coherent way when it touches what's going on in the brain, and clears up some of it. And then from there on, that perception of truth gives rise to thought which can also act in a more coherent way.

Q: You're not separating the truth from 'that which is', are you?

Bohm: No, truth is a part of 'that which is'. Truth is a movement, or act, within 'that which is'. It actually *is*.

Q: Can you say that truth is the action, and has its own actuality?

Bohm: Yes. Truth has its own actuality.

Q: Truth lived would be life without reflex then? Would we be living without the reflex?

Bohm: Truth is not a reflex. It is a creative perception. We need the reflex, but not to be dominated by the reflex.

Q: Can an insight show the truth of how the system works?

Bohm: I'll put it like this: the perception of truth, which may be in a flash of insight, actually changes the system to make it more coherent. And at the same time, it produces the words, or whatever, which communicate a new foundation for thought.

Q: Could that imply that we need coherence to touch the truth?

Bohm: The brain has to quiet down. This incoherence is the source of the electrochemical smog. Our civilization has filled the air with chemical smog, and the lungs are not in condition to breath properly sometimes. Similarly, the brain is not in a condition to respond to truth.

Q: How does it respond to truth then?

Bohm: In this smog, it doesn't; or it responds in a confused way. And therefore it's not truth.

Q: Is truth within the realm of description?

Bohm: No. We're merely trying to give the words which would sort of point there. But it's an actuality. It cannot be described, but it is an actuality which acts. The perception of truth is an actual act which changes things; it's not merely that it is the truth *about* something which is different.

There is also the truth of the false. The truth of the false is not only that it is false; but in the case of the electrochemical smog, for instance, the truth of the false is that it is a material process. Ultimately, underlying the false is the truth.

Q: But the false lies only in abstraction.

Bohm: The false arises through inappropriate abstraction, of a kind which leads to its own defence.

Q: Absolute truth would not be affected by time.

183

Bohm: The truth would not be time. It would not even happen in time. Let's say part of the action of truth is to act on this smog, on the synapses, to remove the incoherence. If it takes time it won't be able to do that, because 'that which is' is changing all the time. And the true perception of one moment would not necessarily hold for the next.

Q: Then truth is revealed in the absence of thought. Might it not be synonymous with beauty and joy?

Bohm: Yes, it might be more or less the same area.

Q: Along those lines, a great work of art, of whatever genre, doesn't just have a correct representation of that which it is representing, but there seems to be something more. Is that truth?

Bohm: In some way, yes. Something like it. There was something more – perception – which goes beyond merely representing things. Though the representation may be there, it's more than that. Perhaps there was a perception of truth when the artist was painting it, or doing it.

Q: And that would be part of the reason why a very repressive kind of totalitarian system would try to restrict and control art.

Bohm: They would not only control and restrict art, but almost anything. They control and restrict science, for example, to whatever areas they think appropriate. They use art just as they use science.

I think perception of truth would only be possible with freedom. So we need to bring in the question of freedom, for which we don't have time now. But truth and freedom must be essentially one field.

Q: Is truth similar to final knowledge?

Bohm: It wouldn't be knowledge though. Truth acts from moment to moment, is what I'm trying to say. Truth is the action from moment to moment.

Q: Is it plain why Einstein held imagination to be so superior to knowledge? He said something like 'Imagination has been infinitely more of service to humankind than is knowledge'.

Bohm: If it's the creative imagination then that's right, because that leads to new perception and to new action.

Q: But since our culture represses that creative imagination in both the arts and sciences we're in a double bind here.

Bohm: Yes, that's why we are going to discuss the culture. I'll just lay some foundation now; then the first part of the afternoon we could discuss culture and dialogue, and go on to the other questions of observer and observed, time and so on.

We have brought up the question of the society and the culture which is suppressing all these things, creating all this smog. The trouble is not primarily originating in the individual, nor is the individual able to handle it entirely by himself. The individual change has tremendous importance; but even if he did change, the change would still have limited meaning. We would still have this whole culture carrying on with the smog. Therefore, unless the whole culture is changed it's not going to have all that deep a meaning. Fundamentally, the whole question of identity, self-image, repression, assumptions and all that, is rising in the culture, which is *shared meaning*. We share all that; it comes in. We may reject some of it and accept some of it, but even to be able to do that is part of the culture. That's all the system. And the culture underlies the system.

I suggest that we'll begin the afternoon, if we may, by discussing the culture and how dialogue can be a way to start to inquire into how the culture is operating in this field that we've been talking about. It's not enough to see all this happening in ourselves because most of it happens between us.

Q: I had a thought a moment ago when you were talking about truth and insight. There's a thing in mathematics called 'factorial', which calculates how many ways you can combine things. If you have three objects, then there's one times two times three, which would be six combinations. The factorial of ten is over three million. The brain has about twenty billion neurons, and if you factorialized twenty billion it would be a number for all intents and purposes which would be infinite. If the brain is in that state of silence where your conditioning and your thinking are not operating, then might there be an infinity or non-limited quality about the brain? Is it in that state that the brain may be in communion or touched by the true nature of truth and insight?

Bohm: If the brain really is not conditioned deeply and all these combinations are free to move around, then it can respond in an infinity of ways and move in relation to truth.

Shall we finish now?

SUNDAY AFTERNOON

Bohm: At the end of the morning session we were saying that all this thought – this whole system – is even more social and cultural than it is individual. And it is necessary to go into that in order to see the whole of it, to see the essential features of it. The way we are proposing to do that is by dialogue. The word 'dialogue' has the root 'dialogos'. In Greek 'dia' means 'through' and 'logos' means 'the word' or 'the meaning'. We may picture meaning flowing between people. 'Dia' doesn't mean 'two' but 'through'. Therefore, many people can participate – it is between us or among us.

One view of relationship would be to look at two people as two points connected by a dotted line showing their relationship as a secondary feature. Another view is a solid line with a point at each end – which is to say that the relationship is the main thing and the people are at the ends, are the extremes of it. And in the dialogue we might perhaps be that way.

Just as thought separates the self into the subject and object, into the observer and the observed – which is all one process – so thought separates people. But when people are really in communication, in some sense a oneness arises between them as much as inside the person.

Of course, 'dialogue' has not been commonly used in that sense. For example, people talk about dialogues in the United Nations; they say things like 'we negotiate'. However, negotiation is only the beginning. If people don't even know how to get started they may trade off various points trying to find out at least how to proceed; but if you merely trade off points and negotiate then that doesn't get very far.

The view of the dialogue which I am suggesting goes very much further than that. I read many, many years ago of an anthropologist who visited a North American Indian tribe of hunter-gatherers. They would meet in a circle of about thirty or forty people, and they would talk directly with each other. Apparently there was no particular authority, though it may be that the older people were more listened to because they were supposed to be wiser. They talked with no agenda, no purpose; they made no decisions and they ended the circle for no apparent reason. And after that they apparently understood each other well enough so that they knew what to do. That was their way of life; they met again and again, in sort of a sustained way.

It seemed to me at that time that this would be the right way to live. But in modern civilization, or even in older ones, we don't appear to be able to do so. People seem to require an authority or hierarchy, or else they make determinate decisions. They don't quite understand each other when they are talking, so they never, really, can maintain this sort of thing.

But it is becoming more and more urgent that people should be able to talk together, because technology is making it dangerous if we cannot. The point is: what does it mean to be able to really communicate, for people to try to talk together?

Suppose we put about four or five people together. That is quite a different situation from having twenty or thirty people together. Four or five people can get to know each other and adjust; they can sort of avoid all the difficult questions. In a way they may be reproducing a more family-type situation; somebody may take on the authority or leadership if they want to do something. But with thirty or forty people, or even twenty, then a new thing comes in: there are many different points of view, and you get something more like a cultural situation of a society.

In society we have a culture. I say a culture is basically a *shared meaning*. Without that shared meaning society will fall apart; it's a kind of cement that holds society together. If people want to get together to do anything things must mean the same to them or they can't do it. It would be at cross purposes if everything had a different meaning for different people.

However, in our society there are many subcultures in which things mean something very different – ethnic subcultures, religious and economic subcultures, educated professions, people in different groups – thousands of different divisions. And if people try to get together, from those groups or even within one of those groups, they may have somebody who runs the thing and then they can try to do what they want. But if they were given a leaderless, agendaless group they probably would feel very anxious and not know what to do. Even if they went through that anxiety, they would find sooner or later that they all had different views and opinions – that they were not communicating, and each one was doing things which were irritating the others, making the others angry. Each one would have a way of thinking which would make the others feel very uncomfortable or exasperated. They start blaming each other for all these things, as I've seen happen, and the whole thing degenerates. They just fall apart; they say 'what's the use?'.

In fact, that kind of difficulty arises whenever people try to get together for a common purpose, whether in the government or in business or wherever. You find that this is the kind of thing that is going on. For instance, the legislators really don't get together in Congress to come to a common meaning; they just trade off certain points in order to pass bills. In contrast, I understand that when the Constitution of the United States was written, the writers spent a long time working together on it in the same place. They hammered it all out so that they would all agree on the Constitution, which was a relatively unified document – though it had certain problems in it which were not unified, such as those which led to the Civil War, and so on.

Now, that's a kind of introduction to the concept of dialogue. And for merely practical purposes we would need dialogue. But in addition it has a much deeper significance, which we will go into later.

If you went through this process, though, you would find difficulties. First of all, some people become dominant. They talk easily and run the show. Others keep quiet, perhaps because they are afraid of making fools of themselves; but they feel somewhat resentful of those who are dominant, and that would also split the group. Some people act out roles, and other people find this very irritating. All sorts of things would be happening. These are all problems which will arise when a group tries to get together, but they are still on the surface.

Suppose we got through all that. Then come more difficult things. People have different basic assumptions about the important things in life – assumptions as to what is really necessary, what is really true, the way people ought to be, what our real purpose ought to be, and all that. And as we've seen, these assumptions are in the form of *reflexes*. People don't quite know they have them. But when the assumptions are challenged, suddenly a person may jump up with an emotional charge. And then it goes back and forth; the whole group can polarize between two such assumptions.

We once tried to hold a dialogue in the early period in Israel, and somebody said very quietly and innocently that the trouble between Jews and Arabs is Zionism – the main trouble is that Zionism keeps them apart. Then suddenly somebody else rose up with his eyes popping out, and said that without Zionism the State would fall to pieces. So there were two different assumptions: one was that it was really necessary to drop this idea of Zionism, and the other was that without it Israel would be impossible. Both were correct in a way, but there was no way to bring them together.

Such assumptions generate tremendous power. They're really assumptions of *necessity*. And what can happen in such cases is that a lot of people are then drawn in who weren't before. In this instance the thing became very heated – full of this electrochemical smog – and the people who hadn't at first been worried about it were all drawn in. But a few were able to deflect it a bit, so it didn't go too far. It didn't get resolved; a dialogue would have to be sustained a long time to resolve a thing like that. However, it did reach the point where the people could at least talk to each other. The fellow didn't walk out, and they were able to listen to some extent to those two opposing assumptions or opinions.

This may seem a small point, but it's really crucial. The world is full of different assumptions of that kind – such as the ones between capitalism and communism which, until recently, divided the world. Each country has assumptions of its sovereignty. And its neighbour has a contrary assumption that it is right and it is sovereign, and so on. These are assumptions all the way through: 'who's the boss', 'I'm the one who runs it'. But somebody else wants to run it: 'I would be better able to do it.' There are so many assumptions, and they are very powerful. They are assumptions of necessity. All the literature and the dramas in the culture contain them; they are in there implicitly. The Greek dramas were full of those assumptions of necessity, which created the tragedies. The hero, who was really a very fine person, very consistently stuck to his assumptions of necessity and thus destroyed himself and everybody around him.

And this is all collective. It's not just an individual thing. There are whole groups who stick together because of this. We pick up these assumptions from the culture. 'Culture' has the same root as 'cultivate'; we sort of cultivate it in some way. The culture contains all these meanings of what is necessary; we have all that.

Now, with any group of people – including this one, if we were to stick at it and meet, say, once a week for an indefinite period; not forever, but indefinitely – in the beginning you would be polite, you would find various topics to talk on about which you could agree. As an example, there was one group where there were some liberal left-wingers on one side and conservatives on the other. They found a lot of things to talk about which had nothing to do with their politics. Then

191

gradually they ran out of those things, and somehow they began to have to talk about the things on which they didn't agree. And then it wasn't so easy.

Sooner or later, in this group or in any group, these types of problems would arise. And if we can't face them then we can't work together. But suppose you have to work together. I'll give a typical problem which some of us have been thinking about recently. The directors or the executive officers of companies need to work together in a group and also with the rest of the company. But each person has a different assumption, which is a kind of reflex, and he doesn't know he has it. Thus, people may be implicitly following different policies and therefore going off in different directions. Although they're supposed to be working together, they are really resisting each other.

The same is true in the government. Clearly the government is full of people resisting one another. They're cancelling each other's efforts and confusing the whole thing. And in every organization you will find that. Even if you set up a chief on top, the others have their own opinions and they won't necessarily follow the directives from the top. They may seem to follow them, but there is a resistance underneath. They are not following him, and he can't get his policies carried out.

So we need an effort to talk. What can we do with this? I'm saying that there is a way – which means dialogue.

It's really the same problem with the individual. We've said that the individual has contrary intentions inside of him, contrary reflexes. Suppose somebody is angry and he wants not to be. He says; 'Being angry is terrible. It's going to destroy what I'm doing, but I'm still angry.' On one hand he has the intention to remain angry and on the other hand he has the intention to stop being angry. The two intentions may be in the same person or in different people, but it operates that way. And if you set up a group, it works much the same.

When we talked about the individual we said that you have to stay with this conflict, you don't escape it. You stay with it, you even bring it out. And you begin to get some insight, you begin to see how thought is producing conflict. As an individual you need to see that staying with this, doing this, is more important than any particular issue you are trying to resolve. In other words, if you can do this you have gone to a deeper level beyond the issues that are disturbing you.

The same is true in the group – we stay with this conflict of intentions, reflexes, assumptions. Every assumption is implicitly a reflex and a set of intentions. And just as happens with the individual, so it moves out into the group. Each person is affected by the other people's thoughts, so that the reflexes of one person become the reflexes of the other. If one person is angry, the other is angry. It all spreads.

Q: Do we have to find a broader common assumption of necessity, a deeper one? When you say that about the individual, I could see where I have a necessity or an intention to understand the process. That necessity may be stronger than the necessity of moving away from my anger.

Bohm: Yes, if you really see it. To see this, though, you must see the meaning of what's going on, the deeper meaning. However, it's not likely that you will see this on the basis of the conditioning we have in society. But we have to go into it, we have to see the deeper meaning of this whole situation. What I want to emphasize here is that the dialogue does not proceed from imposing a purpose or an intention. If we just said 'let's all decide to do this', whatever we might choose to do would be an imposition – it would really be more conflict.

Q: Would people have to come together already having that intention?

Bohm: No, maybe it can develop as we communicate. The

point is that we won't start with a dialogue right away, as we're not starting right now. We start by talking *about* dialogue. We are not pretending that we're having a dialogue. Rather, just as we're talking about all these other things, we start talking about dialogue. We are seeing the meaning. Just as we saw the meaning of the whole thought process and how it's going wrong, we also see the meaning of this situation collectively.

Let's look at this question of *meaning*. The dictionary gives three senses of the word 'meaning'. One of them is 'significance'; it's like a 'sign' that points to something. Another is 'value'. And there is 'purpose' or 'intention'. These are connected, because if you say 'something means a lot to me', you mean it has a high value. And if you say 'I mean to do it', that is the same as to say 'it's my purpose, my intention'. They're related words, obviously. Something with great significance will generate a sense of value. And the value is the energy that infuses you; it makes you feel it's worth doing, or worthwhile.

Q: When you're talking here you are consciously or unconsciously creating a significance.

Bohm: That's the point. I want to say that I'm communicating a significance.

Q: But if I were to get together with a group of people, I might not be able to articulate that significance. It just may not be available.

Bohm: I think that it would. I'm suggesting that we start by communicating this significance and seeing where we can go. If people who have no notion of this whole process of thought and dialogue get together it's possible that they might find a way, but the chances are they would not. Nevertheless, by a creative step they might somehow do it.

194

Q: It seems, though, that there's also another possibility. If they are sufficiently open they may see a common necessity.

Bohm: That may be. But I'm saying that the typical people in our society have reflexes which are against that openness.

Q: We may not have to create or project any significance. We may have a common necessity that we can possibly discover in this process.

Bohm: You can't see necessity without the significance. Necessity is a significance. The situation signifies necessity. It signifies that it cannot be otherwise. So how do you know that something is necessary?

Q: I would say through perception, awareness of it.

Bohm: But that's a significance – you see the meaning of the situation which implies that something is necessary. How do you know what is necessary? Look at a situation: I perceive 'x' is necessary. But that's a certain significance. Necessity and contingency are two significances.

Q: Doesn't the perception give it the significance? Once you have that perception, isn't that the first thing that happens?

Bohm: Yes, it will. But if everybody were perceiving clearly we wouldn't have this problem.

Q: Obviously we're not. But maybe there's a possibility that we could see this common meaning.

Bohm: At some point we may see a common meaning; that's

195

what I'm trying to say. I'm just outlining the idea of meaning now, and saying that at some point we may all see a common meaning – which includes what is necessary, what is valuable, what is worthwhile. And also I'm outlining the purpose and what the intentions are which could realize that. The value and the purpose flow out of the perception of the meaning. Now, the purpose may be changing, because as you see the meaning more deeply you may have to shift the purpose. Is that clear?

I want to show that we have to start by seeing the significance. Perhaps those early people saw the significance easily. But now we have gone through thousands of years of civilization with its smog and what not, and it is very hard to see the meaning of this. Even if we see it by intellect, by inference, it still is not working in the reflexes. In other words, people who see that we need to get together still can't do it, because the reflex comes up – such as Zionism and anti-Zionism.

Q: For me the word 'necessity' has the same meaning as 'meaning'.

Bohm: It's a kind of meaning, but there are very many meanings besides necessity. For instance, there's the general and the particular, there's necessity and contingency. And there are a lot of other things like that. There are many meanings, and necessity is a particular kind of meaning.

Q: Isn't that fundamental to dialogue, though? Isn't there a necessity?

Bohm: That's right, there is a necessity. If we all see the necessity of dialogue we will just be doing it. But I'm starting from a situation where that is not a common perception.

Q: Would you say that the necessity arises out of the meaning, that if you don't understand what it means you can't understand that it's necessary?

Q: That's what I'm questioning, because I think that the necessity is there already. We have this necessity in the way that the world is.

Bohm: But most people don't see it.

Q: They don't see it, they don't see the meaning of that. But isn't it a fact?

Bohm: As you just said, they don't see the meaning. The meaning is what they don't see. The meaning is necessary to see the fact. You don't see the fact clearly unless you see a coherent meaning. What things mean to you will determine the way you act. If something means an enemy, or whatever, you act accordingly. That's what we were saying, that our thinking goes into the perception and gives it a different meaning. So a great deal of thought has gone into perception, giving it a different meaning. And the meaning – which our thought gives it – is that no dialogue is necessary, that we can all go on as individuals doing whatever we like, that the highest form of civilization is every individual doing something just for himself and not consulting anybody else. And that's what almost everybody is saying. In fact, people like Ronald Reagan have said that that's the highest. And Margaret Thatcher prided herself on that. And so on.

Q: Suppose we say we have a given number of facts, such as that various things are happening in the world. For one person that statement means we should go hide in the hills and collect ammunition. For another person it means we should get together and talk.

197

Bohm: And for another person it means forget about it all and just take care of yourself.

Q: Therefore many different meanings could come out of that.

Bohm: Yes, because of all those different thoughts. It may be that if we actually saw it clearly we would see together that we really need dialogue. But there are vast numbers of thoughts which have come in, and they enter into the perception of the meaning. People are seeing the meaning differently, which is why we can't get together.

Q: How would you get people together in the first place? For what reason would they get together if not for this purpose?

Bohm: People are together to a certain extent because they want to do various things. And in addition they might get together for this reason. But people are trying to get together for countless reasons and not succeeding. For example, there are the people who are interested in the ecological crisis. They all have different meanings as to what should be done, and they can fight each other and cancel out each other's efforts. They are trying to get together; but not seeing the point of what's going on – not seeing how thought works – they are not able to.

Q: Are you suggesting that those people could get together for a particular ecological reason?

Bohm: But then they would discover that they cannot do whatever they wanted to do unless they go into this deeper question of meaning. At present there's a danger that the whole ecological movement will split up; in fact it has split up a lot, the same as everything else has split up, because everybody has a different meaning.

Q: Isn't that one step removed from the fact then? We've already given it a particular meaning, whatever the meaning is: how we perceive reality, the world situation, or whatever. Hasn't that moved into a personal or subjective direction away from the fact?

Bohm: It has moved, but the fact is that it has moved. We must start with this fact. The higher order of fact is that people are not looking at the true fact. That's where we have to start – from that fact.

Q: But as you're saying, the circumstances are beginning to compel us to do that in new ways.

Bohm: They're making it necessary to do it, but whether we will do it or not remains to be seen.

Q: Is it important or even necessary to have a reason for a group of people to come together to attempt to have a dialogue?

Bohm: If thirty arbitrarily chosen people just got together they probably wouldn't have a dialogue. I'm trying to say that we have to see the meaning of dialogue, the significance and the value of dialogue, if we are going to sustain the work needed to make it happen. It won't happen in just five minutes. You have to sustain the dialogue week after week, because there are all these resistances that are going to come up. So people will need to have a firm perception of the meaning of dialogue, of the meaning of the whole situation.

Q: But what is this meaning? I've been in many, many of

these groups. Every once in a while I ask 'why are we here?'. Nobody seems to know.

Bohm: I think people do have some vague sense of it, which is not yet formulated; that's one of the difficulties we have to get through. We need a creative step so that we see this firmly. If you have an insight into it, you could then put it in words.

Now, you could ask: 'Why don't people see this clearly? It seems a very present danger and yet it seems people can't see it.' They don't see it because of this thought process, which is collective as well as individual. The thoughts, the fantasies and the collective fantasies are entering perception. Myths are collective fantasies, and every culture has its myths. Many of them are entering perception as if they were perceived realities. Everybody has a somewhat different way in which this happens, and we don't actually see the fact. *That* is the fact: that we don't see the fact. There is a higher order of fact – which is that we are not seeing the direct fact. As I said, that is the fact from which we must start.

Q: If we were to begin to deconstruct our culture, wouldn't we also be able to deconstruct our individual conditioning as we go along? Are they not one and the same?

Bohm: It's the same field – the field of the system of thought. The culture is held together by that system of thought, which has the same flaw, whether it is collective or individual.

Q: Then how do we begin to deconstruct it?

Bohm: I'm discussing that the dialogue will do it. We're sort of trying to get into it.

Suppose we say that we see the meaning of the situation enough to see that it calls for something, it makes something necessary. It makes dialogue necessary. And also we see the value of dialogue, that it is very important. So we're beginning to generate some sort of purpose, at least some immediate purpose of what shall we do. That purpose may change again and again, because as we move along we may want to do something else. What I want to say is that we can't start from the purpose. Rather, we have to start from seeing the meaning. And the perception of the meaning can get deeper and deeper as well.

Now why would we stick together – having all these contrary assumptions and reflexes, and going through all the unpleasantness and frustration? Why would we want to stick together? If something is important, we know we will do it. If we see this is important then we will stick together and say 'let's sustain the dialogue and see if we find creatively how to get through this'.

Q: If we see the necessity of it.

Bohm: That's what the situation means to us, that it is a necessity. To somebody else it may mean it's no necessity at all – 'I can just take care of myself'. I'm proposing that that's because of a certain way of thought. So can we have an insight into the necessity, an insight which really removes this smog? People try to get hold of this, but they get lost in the smog.

Q: The necessity of what?

Bohm: Of really communicating, freely. But these assumptions, for example, are stopping us from communicating. They give this emotional charge; we defend them against evidence that they are wrong, and so on. We need to see the necessity of seeing all of that, including the whole neurophysiological chemical process involved which binds us.

201

Q: Then an ordinary group might not have that necessity?

Bohm: They wouldn't even know about this. How could they see that necessity if they don't know about this at all?

Q: Are you suggesting that it might work with an ordinary group, or it couldn't work with an ordinary group?

Bohm: It's not likely. Possibly if they were very creative and they stuck with it they might find it anyway. I mean, we don't want to put limits on human possibilities. But I'm saying that it doesn't look likely.

Q: More and more, scientists of group process are coming to see and to show people that the biggest obstacle to a group achieving whatever it was formed to do is that it has to share meaning; that in order for a group to be able to do whatever it's going to do, it first needs to learn how to share meaning together.

Bohm: Yes, and that means dialogue. That's what I'm saying.
When we say we see the necessity of sharing meaning, the first thing we discover is that we can't do it. That's the same thing as with the individual – we see the necessity of staying with anger but we can't do it, we're moving away. So then what we have to watch is how we move away. And if we are really serious about it we say: 'I really see the necessity, and I won't just stop because I failed at that point. I'll stick with it and see if I can't find why it's not working.'

Q: One can sort of play with it.

Bohm: You can play with this, but then you will get frustration because very serious assumptions will come up which

are very, very, powerful. You have to say that you'll stick
with it even though it gets difficult and unpleasant.

We can't guarantee that this is going to work. But we can't
guarantee that any other difficult thing you might want to
do is going to work either. If you ask for a guarantee before-
hand you might never do it.

Q: In a way we don't even know what 'working' means. We
may think it's supposed to work in a certain way, and it may
be working differently on a level we have no idea about.

Bohm: Yes, we don't know too well what it means.

Now let me give what I call 'a vision of dialogue' to sort
of paint an idea of what it might mean. You don't have to
accept it, but it may be a way to look at it. I'm not saying
that what we're envisioning will work, not right away at any
rate. It may be that when you first try this it won't work. But
still, it's an important vision. Almost anything worthwhile
doesn't work when you first try it.

Let's suppose we can stick with this. And we face this
emotional charge – all this smog, all this irritation, all this
frustration – which can actually develop into hate if very
powerful assumptions are there. The smog between the Zion-
ist and the anti-Zionist could easily do that, and that's rather
mild compared with what is really possible with some
assumptions. We could say that hate is a neurophysiological
chemical disturbance of a very powerful kind, which is now
endemic in the world. Wherever you look, you see people
hating each other. So suppose you stick with this. You may
get an insight, a shared insight, that we're all in the same
position – everybody has an assumption, everybody is stick-
ing to his assumption, everybody is disturbed neurochemically. The fundamental level in people is the same; the
superficial differences are not so important.

I am presenting this as an inference. But if you actually get
an insight, at that moment it might touch the whole reflex

structure with all the chemistry. It might be touched at that moment.

It's possible to see that there's a kind of level of contact in the group anyway. The thought process is an extension of the body process, and all the body language is showing it, and so on. People are really in a rather close contact – hate is an extremely close bond. I remember somebody saying that when people are really in close contact, talking about something which is very important to them, their whole bodies are involved – their hearts, their adrenalin, all the neurochemicals, everything. They are in far closer contact with each other than with some parts of their own bodies, such as their toes. So, in some sense there is established in that contact 'one body'. And also, if we can all listen to each other's opinions, and suspend them without judging them, and your opinion is on the same basis as anybody else's, then we all have 'one mind' because we have the *same content* – all the opinions, all the assumptions. At that moment the difference is secondary.

The point then is that you have in some sense one body, one mind. It does not overwhelm the individual. If the individual has another assumption he can have it, it's shared with the group and the group takes it up. There is no conflict in the fact that the individual does not agree. It's not all that important whether you agree or not. There is no pressure to agree or disagree.

Q: Are you saying that there's contact, but the thoughts which people have might be quite different – there doesn't need to be an agreement?

Bohm: We don't have to agree that somebody is right, but we have to listen to every thought and see its meaning.

Q: Then the connection is molecular, it's not in thought.

Bohm: It's sort of molecular. It's hard to describe; I mean, it is at another level. In early times they had it quite frequently. And I think people want that very much.

In England, for example, the football crowds prefer not to have seats in their football stands, but just to stand bunched against each other. There are so many people, and when something exciting happens they push against each other and sometimes people get killed because of the crowd. They can't control it any more, and the pressure builds up to something where people can't breathe. There was a recent incident where a lot of people were killed. And there have been other incidents of that nature. So some people began to suggest 'why not put seats in all these football stands?'. But many other people objected. They said: 'We don't want seats. We want that contact.' The reason they're going to those football games is not just to see the games; the game is a socially acceptable reason for having this contact which the society doesn't allow anywhere else.

Q: If I can look beyond the assumptions – respect yours and have my own – then can I see me in you?

Bohm: We can see that we all have these assumptions. and we look at all the assumptions. I'm looking at your assumptions and my assumptions. They're all suspended. I'm not deciding they are right or wrong. Or, if I think I prefer mine, well, that's OK. But still I'm looking at the meaning of what you say. And therefore we are sharing a common meaning. Then, if somebody else comes up with another assumption we all listen to that; we share that meaning. Now that would be the 'vision of dialogue'.

The point is that we would establish on another level this kind of bond, which is called impersonal fellowship. You don't have to know each other. In those football crowds very few people know each other, but they still feel something – that contact – which is missing in their ordinary personal relations. And in war many people feel that there's a kind of

205

comradeship which they miss in peacetime. It's the same sort of thing – that close connection, that fellowship, that mutual participation.

I think people find this lacking in our society, which glorifies the separate individual. The communists were trying to establish something else, but they completely failed in a very miserable way. Now a lot of them have adopted the same values as we have. But people are not entirely happy with that. They feel isolated. Even those who succeed feel isolated, feel there's another side they are missing.

Q: We're presently talking about dialogue. Don't we have the task at hand, that when we go back home we want to draw people together to dialogue?

Bohm: The suggestion is that we shouldn't think of it as a task. The whole point of dialogue is that we are not going to have an agenda or purpose. We are going to *see* the meaning and act accordingly.

Q: Isn't there still the fact of thirty or forty people coming together under one roof, as we've done here? Something must make that happen.

Bohm: But we can't 'make' it happen, not force it to happen anyway. I'm trying to say that we can only look, as we did with the individual. We can only *perceive* the situation. And our insight may change the barriers to this.

Q: So obviously there's no prescription; that would be a contradiction to what we're talking about. Yet there is something unknown that must be done – which can or cannot be done – for this to happen.

Bohm: Yes, something must happen, and we don't know

whether it will or not. What I'm trying to present is the *meaning* of dialogue – a 'vision of dialogue'. By seeing the meaning we will then begin to feel the value of it and begin to establish purposes, which may help bring us towards it.

Q: The more the meaning, the more the action?

Bohm: From the meaning flows the sense of value. And from that flows the purpose and the action.

Q: Are we talking about a shift in emphasis of priorities and importance? Could we see the importance of communication, and see that staying with the fact is more important than our own assumptions? And do we try to bring that idea into situations?

Bohm: If we once see the importance it will come. Therefore we have to ask 'if we've seen the importance, why aren't we doing it?' The answer is always 'there is further chemistry and there are further reflexes which we haven't touched'.

Q: Then it's something we could work on?

Bohm: Yes. By sustaining the dialogue we are beginning to probe into all that deeper chemistry which was hidden. And part of the whole process of these reflexes is to hide themselves, so as to avoid disturbing the apple cart. I'm suggesting that if we try to realize this 'vision of dialogue' we may find that we can't do it. But every 'vision' has that character at first.

So we have to sustain the dialogue in spite of frustration and all the troubles. This energy of frustration and hate, and the rest, would be dispelled and released as fellowship. There is some close bond in that frustration, but now it could become a different kind. When people are engaged in the opposition of deep assumptions, there is a close bond between them. If they're indifferent to each other or if they're politely avoiding the issue, it isn't there.

If you stay with this it creates a possibility of a certain change. It's very similar to what you have to do in the individual problem – to stay with the difficult situation, not escape it. If you find yourself escaping you need to watch yourself escaping, and so on. It's like the question of sorrow, which Krishnamurti talked about a lot – that faced with sorrow people seek a constant escape, a constant movement away from awareness of it. The reflexes try to relieve the situation by moving you away. And that means you could never find out what it is, what's going on; you could never perceive that. But if you see yourself moving away and stay with that, that staying with it builds up a great deal of energy. The more you stay with it, the more you get a sense that it's all really some sort of physical tension. Then you may get an insight that this whole thing is just a part of the material process.

The social problem is also part of the material process, but we give it a very different significance. For instance, people don't think that the problem between nations is part of the material process; rather, it's given a transcendental significance. But, actually, it is just the material process which has become muddled up – it's in this smog situation. In a moment of insight in the group we may see that we share this material process, and that this material process we share is more significant than all the particular thoughts where we differ.

Q: Would you say that the sustaining of the dialogue within oneself increases the possibility of the dialogue with others?

Bohm: Yes, because once you have an insight into this, sustaining the dialogue in yourself will help the others. Or, sustaining the dialogue with the others will help the individual, and help also communication outside the group. And the people who understand this could then try to establish dialogue groups, and so on.

Usually for such a dialogue group there should be a facilitator to help get it going and help point out what's going on, and so forth, who gradually becomes less and less necessary. He might have the 'vision of dialogue', which he could communicate. It's important that the group see the meaning of dialogue and have this sort of vision of it, to keep going and to keep on developing that. The group may talk about dialogue again from time to time, but it would not be worthwhile to keep on asking 'are we having a dialogue?'. Although sometimes it is worthwhile.

I think now would be a good point to have a break.

Bohm: We've been discussing dialogue, to give the meaning and to give a 'vision of dialogue'. Tomorrow, those who stay will try to begin something of a dialogue throughout the day. But I think in the remaining time today we'd like to discuss a few other points which we always consider in these seminars.

One of the points is this question of *separation*. Once we form the thought of separation – the image and the imagination of separation – we perceive things and people as separate. Then we make them separate, as when we draw a line between countries and perceive two countries and we then create two countries.

So we could say that though our bodies are individual, nevertheless they are capable of a close connection on another level through communication, which we've talked about. The thought process is a fundamentally collective system anyway. You would not have it in its present form except through a culture and a society. A language could only exist that way.

The individuality that we have – or that we think we have – is to a large extent the product of our culture, which creates the particular image of the individual. But all the people in a certain culture have more or less the same image of their individuality. It's clear that thought determines the question of what is connected or separate, how you see it, and so on.

In our personal consciousness there is the impression that

209

there is an observer and an observed, there is a thinker who produces thoughts separate from himself. And once thought has formed the image of the self as 'me' and 'I', then there is the view that it is 'I' who creates thought. In other words, thought has explained its origin through the image by attributing itself to that image, just as you could attribute the sound of the telephone to the image in the television set and feel it to be there. In a similar way, the feeling could be created that somewhere in the head is the source of thought.

Also, you have the division between the self and the world. You say: 'I end at my skin. Outside is the world.' And you experience it that way. But that experience can be very variable. There's the example of a blind man with a stick. If he holds the stick tightly he may feel that he ends at the end of the stick; but if he loosens his hold, then he may feel that he ends at his fingertips. Similarly, if a person identifies himself as part of a country he may feel that he ends at the boundary of his country, and if somebody crosses the boundary he feels attacked. Or you may feel you are one with the universe. Or vice versa, you have the opposite sense – the thought which tries to go inward, inward to the very essence, the core of the self, down to one point, thinking that that point is 'me' and the rest is being observed by me.

But it's all an image. It changes around according to the situation. That image may be more correct or less correct in various situations. Where the connection is close it may be a correct representation, and where it's loose it is not. So it would require seeing the coherence of that to see how it works in each case.

We have this notion, then, that the agent, the thinker, creates the thought. And a person may identify himself with almost anything. Descartes said 'I think, therefore I am', which meant his essential being was in the action of thinking – he felt that the action defined his being. And many people may feel that way from time to time.

Now, we're suggesting that thought is a system belonging to the whole culture and society, evolving over history, and it creates the image of an individual who is supposed to be the source of thought. It gives the sense of an individual who is perceived and experienced, and so on. This would be conducive to the next step, which is for thought to claim that it only tells you the way things are and then the individual inside decides what to do with the information – he chooses. This is the picture which emerged gradually: thought tells you the way things are and then 'you' choose how to act from that information.

Q: But does thought really tell you how things are? I think thought distorts it. Only observation without the observer can tell you how things really are, because the thinker can manipulate thought and then he sees what he wants to see.

Bohm: I said only that in this picture or image, thought claims to be telling you the way things are. That is not to say that they are the way it tells you. To a certain extent it gives valuable information, when it's working right. But thought says 'this is the way things are, and you – the thinker – must decide what to do'. And that's all misinformation according to what we're saying.

Let's say that you have an image of yourself as good and something happens – perhaps your friend doesn't back up that image. You feel hurt. That image is removed and you're disturbed; and after that moment of disturbance there arises the thought: 'What happened? I'm hurt.' Instead of the pleasure which was in the image, the reflex is pain.

What has happened is that the thought has now separated itself in two and says: 'There is "me" who is hurt. And there is "I", who am the observer, looking at the hurt.' This will create a conflict because the minute you think that, it's implied that the one who is looking will try to stop the hurt and will fight it. But we're saying that that won't work, because there is actually nothing but a process of thought which creates the image of 'I' and 'me'. They are both the same ground really – namely, thought. They are all one.

211

Q: It's interesting that the 'me' has been hurt, but 'I' am going to take revenge. It's like two separate things.

Bohm: Usually what first happens is that the 'me' has been hurt and 'I' must remove or get rid of the pain. 'What can I do?' That's the first reaction. So you start a train of thought: 'Who did it? Who's to blame?' And you say: 'OK, that one's to blame. I must take revenge.' That would be one way out. Or, 'that person must apologize'. Or else another reaction would be to say, 'I should not be hurt'. But then there's a conflict, because the same thought process which makes you be hurt is also fighting and saying you should not be hurt.

Thus, you have these two situations, these two movements. It's really all one, but there is that apparent division which has been built up by this process of thought. We have a representation of the self as capable of being the observer and the observed. Just as we say 'I can look at my body', so we say 'I can look inside and see that it's been hurt'. That analogy is drawn, but it doesn't work. The process in which I look at my body has a certain meaning; but the process in which there is an observer who steps back to look at the hurt inside has no meaning, because it's just two images. It might as well be going on in a television screen. It's like the rainbow, which is really not there but has a real process behind it – rain and light.

So there is a process behind all this, creating this sense of an observer who is supposed to do something. That observer apparently is perceived. And then thought comes along, takes that as if it were a fact, and proceeds to try to overcome the hurt. Whereas if that thought stopped, there would be no problem. Children have a saying: 'sticks and stones can break my bones but words can never hurt me.' It may be true in a sense, but it doesn't work. People still get hurt by names because of the thought which creates the image, which produces either pleasure or hurt.

Now, in so far as you have the image or fantasy which gives pleasure, that same fantasy turns around to give pain

212

when the opposite information gets into it. You are very vulnerable once you depend on fantasy or image to give pleasure, because that creates the sense of 'me', and then comes the division – when the pleasure doesn't work and the struggle and the fight and conflict, and so on. If that division did not occur there would be no conflict.

Actually, no real division occurs, but as I've already said, the appearance of division takes place in the image. If there were no such appearance of division there would be no occasion for conflict. There would be a perception that this is thought. There would be proprioception of thought, expressed in words as: 'this is a train of thought which produces pain.' Then thought would just stop, because you don't want the pain.

But there are all sorts of assumptions, such as: 'I am too important to give up on this thought. I can't allow myself to give up the pain.' Is that assumption clear? It's a common one. People who are hurt have an assumption: 'I can't allow myself to give up that pain because then I would be sort of negating myself, saying that I have no importance. That cannot be allowed. It's absolutely necessary to maintain my importance.'

If we had an insight right away into all this – that the observer *is* the observed, as Krishnamurti so often said – then it would all evaporate. The point is that we have a resistance to that insight. We have the fact that there is confusion and incoherence. And we have the fact that we do not have perception which sees what is going on. There is this chemistry, this reflex, which keeps people going in the same way. The chemistry is affected by the division, and the division is sustained by the chemistry because the body now demands relief. Being disturbed by the chemistry, the body demands relief.

Suppose you hurt your arm. You would notice a disturbance and say 'I feel pain'. And then the thought would come up and say 'what's the cause of the disturbance?'. So you would sort of step back in your mind and look, and say: 'OK, I see that my arm has been hurt. I must do something.'

That would make sense, because the thought and the arm are not really that closely connected. But when it comes to the psychological pain it doesn't make sense.

Q: Would there first be a body image formed?

Bohm: The body image is always there in some sense. We always sense our body.

Q: But you're not talking about the physical image, you're talking of a different image?

Bohm: Yes. We form a self-image. It's very vague, it doesn't have to be well defined. It's just 'me'. You may point to yourself as being in the head or chest or solar plexus or somewhere. You feel somewhere inside is a point or a small region where 'you' are, which is the centre.

Q: Would that image be how we are defined by our parents, by the teacher, by the culture?

Bohm: All of that creates the image and therefore all that content is attributed to the image. Just as the ringing of the bell is attributed to the telephone in the television image, we experience all of this content as existing within the image. The image, however, is perceived as real.

Q: It appears that we exist in that image.

Bohm: All our properties and qualities are in that image. We feel that they are there. If you're hurt you will feel that there really is something inside which has been hurt. People say, 'my heart has been broken'. And in fact they feel something,

214

because in the region of the chest or the solar plexus there is clearly a great disturbance.

Q: So as we continue to grow up and go to school and marry, and whatever, we're adding to the image?

Bohm: Yes. Society is adding to it, saying that you are this sort of person, you are that sort, you should be this, and so on. And you are also adding, you're doing your bit in it. It all adds to build up the image. And that image then reacts; it's made up of a set of reflexes which act according to the image. If the image is that 'I am great', then the action is that 'I would like to hear people say that'. Or else I would say it to myself or try to do something to prove it.

Q: Then it's always going to be a sense of incompleteness?

Bohm: It is always sensed as incomplete, yes, because it's only an image – it could never be complete.

Q: What about the cultural image? Doesn't our culture have its own self-image?

Bohm: It's full of self-images and they are all contradicting each other, just as our individual self-images contradict each other.

Q: Then the individual image and the cultural image are not really two distinct things?

Bohm: Our individual self-images mostly come from the culture. The word 'idiosyncrasy' has the Greek root meaning 'private mixture'. There is a big mixture of images floating around in the culture from which everybody picks his own

215

mixture. Each individual selects images for one reason or another. He doesn't do it consciously. He picks up some of the images and repels some of the others; he finds others revolting, and so on.

Q: Even our sexual images as a man, as a woman?

Bohm: Yes, it is all influenced heavily by the culture, very strongly. It's all there, and we form this image. We have the image that 'I do the thinking', 'I am the thinker'. But in fact the culture has produced most of the thought. It sort of passes through me, I add a bit to it, I do this or that to it. The kind of thought we use, which is communicated, originates basically in the whole society and the culture. We have the sense of separation because our culture tells us that each individual is separate, and therefore we perceive it that way.

Q: It seems very hard not to feel that we are separate, since we're separate within our own skins and we can move around. It's just a very difficult concept to transcend.

Bohm: Yes, because the body actually has this relative independence. But even then, as we said, it's possible for a group to become one body. And people really want that. In the football crowds they are ready to risk life to have it. So it is possible to have the body as individual or the body as a group. But when it comes to the mind, we have become so used to the notion that the mind is individual that we don't notice the plain evidence, all the evidence from which you could infer that it is not.

There is, however, an element of individuality. In so far as there is insight into, let's say, the actual physical neurochemical process we are talking about, that would really be closest to individuality. We could say that something of possibly *cosmic* origin operates directly in the body when there is insight. And perhaps that is the closest we would get to true individuality.

The word 'individual' literally means 'undivided'. But we've seen that the individual which society puts together is highly divided and in conflict. So the question is not clear about what is individual. There is a great deal of incoherence there. And also, the failure to see that some of these distinctions are merely 'dotted lines' leads to a wrong meaning, it leads to endless confusion.

Now, that might raise the question of what kind of *freedom* there is for the person. As long as we are in this system, there is very little freedom. You can say 'I do what I want', but what you want is the result of the system. We are wanting things which are incoherent and creating misery. And we're not free to give that up.

Q: We think we are free when we do what we want, especially when we're young and we don't realize that the want itself prevents freedom.

Bohm: The want comes from the conditioning.

Q: Is what you're talking about freedom of choice, not choice-less freedom?

Bohm: Well, freedom at that level is not very significant. The question is: could freedom have a deeper meaning? I think this is connected with the question of necessity. We may see necessity as external, that certain things are necessary – necessity won't be turned aside, and we have to turn aside or it crushes us. But we have our own internal necessity which may conflict with that, and then we have a struggle. The external necessity may be too powerful and you get crushed; or you may try to dominate and impose your own necessity. That's the sort of pattern we take. We think that to

217

be able to impose our own necessity is freedom; but in fact I'm saying that's still part of the same system.

So we have to get clear on necessity and contingency. Freedom would require some contingency, in the sense that if things couldn't be otherwise then there would be no freedom. But freedom would also require some necessity, because if there were no necessity our intentions would have no meaning. We might intend to do something, but if nothing holds with any necessity then anything may happen, no matter what we intend. Therefore, in some way both necessity and contingency are involved in freedom.

Q: I didn't understand what you just said about necessity and contingency.

Bohm: Necessity is what cannot be otherwise and contingency is what can be. It's because things can be otherwise that you are possibly free to do various things. But if things were totally contingent you would not have any freedom, you wouldn't be able to count on anything. I couldn't count on the necessity of this table to remain a table. I could say 'I want to put the cup on the table', but meanwhile the table might turn into a cloud of gas. So in some way which is hard to express, freedom requires both necessity and contingency.

Q: Then contingency is not the same thing as choice, is it?

Bohm: No, contingency really means 'it can be otherwise'.

Q: Whereas choice is something that's produced in the mind – an image or images of alternatives which the mind thinks it has?

Bohm: Between possibilities you may choose, saying 'I prefer this to that'.

Q: But does it have a base in reality? It's just an image produced by the mind.

Bohm: You may have several alternatives which are correct; there may be several possible roads to go to a certain place. Or suppose I come to a crossroads. One road will take me here, one will take me there; if I choose this road I'll go here, and if I choose that road I will go there. Thus if I want to go there, I should choose that road.

Q: It's all a kind of fiction in a way, because that sort of implies there's something that chooses.

Bohm: That's the language we use. I could put it that if my intention is to go there, I must pick this road. Thought could tell me that correctly. If I want to go there I must go on that road, but if I want to go somewhere else I must go on another road. Thought tells me that. Those are the alternatives.

Q: To get where you're supposed to be going, though, you can only take one turn. I mean, there's action in reality and there is choice in the realm of images. Aren't they two different things?

Bohm: Yes, but I'm saying that the presentation of alternatives is a correct representation that thought could give. But when you say that you choose this alternative, it's not clear what it means — who chooses, or what chooses, or how it gets chosen. Even if that were free, it would seem that it's not a very significant kind of freedom. It does seem that it is not free, however, because if your choice is conditioned then you are not free.

I'm trying to say that freedom may be something deeper. We might think of an artist, a creative artist, who is creating

219

a work of art. There are many possible contingencies – ways of putting his materials here or there and with different techniques. It's open. That's the field in which he can work. And then from some perception – by some sense of internal necessity, some creative perception of necessity – he must begin to develop how this is to be done. Otherwise it won't hold together, it won't have any value or any meaning. In other words, freedom is the *creative* perception of a new order of necessity.

Q: But oddly enough, that necessity isn't anything I 'have'. It's more like: 'Oh, I'm sitting in this chair. How interesting.' I mean, it isn't something I know, or move from.

Bohm: Well, really it's creative. And that creation can also enter into science and technology, and create all sorts of things. In fact, everything that we've created came about ultimately in that way. I'm saying that freedom is the perception and creation of a new order of necessity.

In this way we would say that necessity is involved in freedom. In other words, we don't get free of necessity but freedom is first. One of our pictures is that necessity is getting in the way of our freedom, that if we're stuck by necessity we are not free. If we are bound by four walls then we can't get out. That's one of the views we have – that necessity is external.

Q: It seems to me that in a sense all one can ever be free to do is be an innocent bystander. One really can't do anything other than that.

Bohm: But still you are deeply involved in this creative act. You don't control the creative act. It's coming from the same source as insight.

Q: Saint Augustine said 'Let go, and let God'.

Bohm: That implies that people saw this unconditioned source as God. People may give it various names at various times.

Q: I'd still like to consider contingency and necessity in general. Would this be an illustration that makes any sense? I was listening to a chamber music concert of some very new music. It sounded as if the composer had chosen things with total contingency; but after listening for a while, there began to be a certain inevitability so that after each note the next note made sense. Even though I couldn't conceptualize the pattern, there seemed to be some necessity coming through.

Bohm: If he was a genuine artist, there was a necessity behind it. When somebody comes out with a new order of necessity, other people may not see it right away and it looks to them just like contingency. So they say 'this is rubbish'. In many cases it may be rubbish, but then occasionally it isn't.

Q: Can necessity be felt by an impulse, an impetus?

Bohm: It's felt that way, but also that feeling could come from the conditioning as well. Mozart himself said that he saw the whole composition all at once. Somehow he saw the whole necessity of it, and then he sort of unfolded it. If that was the case, it was a kind of gigantic flash of insight that created the whole thing. And you can't say where it comes from. The same as with any insight, having been created it affects the brain and then the brain works it out – how to play the music, the individual notes, and so on.

This suggests that there is a tremendous potential for creativity; and that we could not only have the creation of new orders of necessity in art or in science, but that maybe we should look at culture, society and ourselves in the same way – look at it as an art, a creative art. The dialogue is

221

potentially a creative art; namely, new orders of necessity may arise if we sustain it.

I don't know how easily it came to Mozart, but they say that to Beethoven it was more of a struggle. He had to sustain this work. And if we sustain a dialogue very seriously, then it becomes possible that there will be something creative and new – which would be the microcosm, the germ, that could then communicate it. In other words, that which appears to be just a lot of meaningless contingency is the field in which some new order of creative necessity might come. And out of that can come a new culture, a new society.

That is the suggestion I want to make: that this notion of artistic, scientific creativity should be extended into all these areas, rather than fragmenting and saying 'it is valid here, but there we go the old way'.

Q: This suggests that necessity is nothing that I have, but rather I place myself at the disposal of necessity. People really can't know what they're supposed to do when they come to a dialogue group, but in some sense they are 'available'.

Bohm: That creative necessity arises in this movement between them. And as with Mozart – in a way you could say that he didn't do this thing, it just happened to him.

Q: Would the meaning that is shared be the necessity?

Bohm: It includes the necessity. To begin with, the meaning is the necessity of dialogue. But when we get through all these barriers which we've been talking about, then maybe with the free flow of communication, with that sense of one-ness, another order of necessity could arise which was altogether. Do you see what I'm driving at? It would be a kind of artistic creation, but it would have the rigour of scientific thought as well.

222

Q: If the new society once took hold, would there ever be no need for dialogue?

Bohm: The dialogue might become natural, in the sense of those early people who just got together and talked.

Q: What I'm trying to ask is: if that pollution within the system is ended, would the system then operate without a need for dialogue?

Bohm: We wouldn't need formal dialogue, but we would still need to talk. Pollution is liable to arise. But if we are very clear and sharp and rapid about it, it won't get very far.

Q: How about individual dialogue? The more the deconditioning comes about, is there less need for dialogue?

Bohm: We wouldn't need dialogue as a way of repairing, but rather communication would take place as a creative act – like the art of communication. In other words, we wouldn't be getting together primarily for the sake of overcoming or dealing with all the mess, rather it would have another meaning.

Q: In the beginning of dialogue, isn't there going to be a lot of pollution?

Bohm: Yes. I'm saying we have to go through that, because we've got it.

Q: You're saying that when we're starting dialogue, we need to let the pollution come out. The aim doesn't seem to be to get rid of incoherence immediately – rather, to let it emerge.

Bohm: Yes, let it come out. We can't get rid of it, any more than Mozart could somehow force that perception to happen.

Q: Actually you don't need to let it come out – it comes out by itself.

Q: No, we usually stop it if it's coming out.

Bohm: Even then, 'we' don't stop it. It's the reflexes which stop it. But thought is always saying that thought didn't do it. It says 'you did it'.

Q: Could we put it that, in the process of dialogue people would start seeing the incongruence and the incoherence of thought? They would realize that it's a lot of defence and protection of the image – a lot of pretending? As that drops, people open themselves up for something different to come through. And it can unfold to each person in different ways.

Bohm: The brain and the system open up to something different. That difference can be something of creative significance, even of cosmic significance – possibly contact with something beyond just the culture and the society.

Q: But you're required to move out of the incoherence.

Bohm: Yes, because all that incoherence muddles up the brain, it creates the smog. The brain is not able to work right. It's poisoned in some way.

The brain is a material system, but it is infinitely subtle and can respond to the creative. If one brain such as Mozart's could do this, it suggests that it should be a potential in general – not necessarily in music, but somewhere, in some field. Mozart may have had some unusual talent or structure which was good for music; but that creative potential, which isn't restricted to any particular field, should be available to everybody within whatever he can do. And it would be important for people to see that. I think that the more civilization has developed, the more it had tended to focus on all these other things – saying that creativity is primarily for the sake of the economy or to provide entertainment, or for some other purpose like that.

So that is the suggestion: that there could arise a freedom which is collective as well as individual. We are not free at all, as long as we are stuck with all this stuff.

Q: And a culture which wants to dominate its citizens will, of course, not encourage creativity, because they don't want people to be creative.

Bohm: The culture wants to defend itself. And we say all of that really looms very large. But actually it's a very small thing. It is something very insubstantial – just very ephemeral thoughts which are circulating all over the society.

Q: Think of how many cultures and empires have collapsed in the history of the world. Maybe this is the time that the cultures are collectively collapsing, and a new culture, a new order is coming up. Maybe this is the microcosm of what is happening.

Bohm: It could be. We don't know for sure. But the point is: the new culture will arise first by our seeing the meaning of this whole situation and seeing the value of it. And then the particular purposes as to what we have to do will emerge as we go along – one purpose after another, rather than starting with a purpose which is fixed.

Q: I want to ask: isn't there only one energy? It's an illusion

that the energy of love is different from the energy of violence. It's the same energy, only in violence it is polluted.
This division creates violence. If we condemn violence, or its
opposite non-violence, that condemnation is merely an idea.
The thought creates the image and the division. But if there
is no division, then this energy in violence is set free – it
transforms.

Bohm: That's true. We're saying that the people in a situation
of hate and violence are in a situation connecting them with
a lot of energy. And this can transform into another kind,
which is friendship and fellowship and love. But that requires
that we take this seriously and really sustain the work of
communicating – of dialogue – if we are going to be able to
do it together.

And it's essential to do this together because as an individual it will have a limited meaning. Doing it together
means that we're communicating, facing all these issues and
whatever happens – persisting and sustaining the work even
when it becomes difficult and unpleasant. The fact is we are
violent, we have all that. To imagine we don't have it will be
meaningless. So we have to say that we have it. And we
have to stay with it. We perceive it. We need to perceive the
real meaning of it, which is that we are bound together by
this physical thing which we call 'violence'.

Q: It seems that we see appearances differently and we see
ourselves as separate because our awareness is incoherent.
But once we go into this it becomes coherent and extremely
powerful.

Bohm: It is very powerful because it's all working together
instead of being in different directions. It doesn't cancel out
but it works together. I sometimes give the example of a
laser. Ordinary light waves are called 'incoherent'; they go in
all directions and are not in phase with each other, so they

don't build up. But the light coming from a laser is coherent, because the waves all beam in the same direction and build up great strength. Similarly, if even a few people were to think together in a coherent way it would have tremendous power in the culture and in the society.

Now, one of the questions that's involved in all this is *time*. All thought involves time, in a way which we don't see. We tend to think that everything exists in time, that time is an independent reality. People represent time by space. In a diagram they draw a line and call it 'time', and say that here is a point in time, which is now, then another point, then another point. Clearly, thought is then representing time through space.

But we seem also to experience time psychologically. Leibniz, the philosopher, has said that space is the order of co-existence. All that co-exists is in a certain order which we call 'space'. And time is the order of successive existence – the order of *succession*. The real basis of time is succession – things succeeding each other in a certain order. Time is a concept which is set up by thought to represent succession.

All sorts of concepts of time are possible. In the early days people didn't think much about time. They may have had a vague notion of past and future – the vague notion of tomorrow being any time, and the past not remembered very well. There were no printed records. The past was mostly mythological; and the future was probably equally mythological, if they thought of it at all. They could possibly have thought of seasons and things like that. The seasons are the succession of process. Your body goes through a succession of rhythms. And that succession is the basis of the whole thing – that is a thing that's actual.

Thought deals with that, puts it in order by means of the concept of time. We may draw a line and call that 'time', but as I have said earlier, that's really representing time by space. You say the clock tells time, but it doesn't. What you actually see is the position of the hands of the clock, not the time. It means time; it's been set up in such a way that it should measure time. But we never actually see, perceive, or experience 'time' – it's inferred.

227

Nevertheless, we seem somehow to experience time in our own psychological existence. But if you thought that time was a basic reality then you would have a paradox. The past is gone – it doesn't exist. The future doesn't exist either – it's not yet. And the present, if it were thought of as the point dividing past and future, also could not exist, because it would be dividing what doesn't exist from what doesn't exist. That's the paradox of this view. However, it is no paradox if you just say that *time is a representation*. A representation can be all kinds of things.

Science has developed all sorts of notions of time. There is Newton's idea of absolute time – a certain moment that's the same for the whole universe, and then another moment succeeding it, and then another one. Einstein challenged that, and said time is relative to speed, and so on.

You can change the ideas of time and of space, but they are all representations. Each one may have a domain where it's correct; and beyond that it may not be right, may not work coherently. But in our culture we have a tacit assumption that everything exists in time.

Q: We make the mistake of using time in the psychological field. Somebody may say that he needs many years to become transformed. But that's a very dangerous mistake, because you never know when insight may happen. I don't think that time has a place in the psychological field.

Bohm: Yes, but why is it that it *seems* to have a place? Thought has assumed time and has represented time as the essence of existence. We say, 'time is of the essence'. But if we say that time is of the essence, then time must be the 'being' – what we are. And from that thought, which is a commonly accepted notion, comes the perception that time is the essence. Whether time really is the essence or not is irrelevant, because once it's commonly accepted we *perceive* it that way. Then it becomes an absolute necessity.

Q: Time is one of the measurables – what we call 'substances'. We measure time, count on it, predict the space between today and tomorrow. We make predictions on it based on our experience between today and yesterday, and count on the same rhythm. So it seems to have some substance. And it's quite useful, such as for measuring distance or form or something like that. Therefore, it does seem to be one of the essences of our existence.

Bohm: It may appear to be so. You were discussing evidence in favour of its being the essence, but the point is that it is nevertheless an abstraction. We can say that as an abstraction or as a representation it may operate correctly in a certain domain – it keeps track of succession.

Q: Are you saying that time and space are one?

Bohm: They may be one. The theory of relativity implies their unity. Measurement of time and space keeps track of the order of succession in a process. But you first have the order of succession, and then you have the concept of time. Now, however, it seems to have turned around – it seems that you first have time, and in that time succession takes place.

Q: And you're saying that if we lose track of the fact that it's a representation, it can become problematic?

Bohm: Yes, or confusing or incoherent. There is the same problem as with all thought: the representation enters perception and seems to be an actual fact. And the rest of thinking then takes that as proof, and then proceeds to go on from there. It starts to erect all sorts of things on a wrong foundation.

I'm saying that before we can think of psychological time,

229

we need to see that the very notion of time itself is misunderstood. Even in physics it is not adequately being understood as an abstraction, as a representation. In a certain area this will not be too important, because physical processes are regular enough that they can be measured by time. Therefore, even though you have this misunderstanding you are not going to come to a serious practical incoherence. For instance, if we have all timed our watches together and we say that we are going to meet at a certain time, then, if our watches work properly, we will be in the same place. If they don't work properly we will not.

So you can see that, physically, the concept of time implies that there is a great order of nature in the whole universe. From the most distant stars to here, every atom vibrates at a certain rate which is the same as it is here. There are all sorts of regularity that constitute a vast system of order, which the concept of time is tapping into, as it were. If that order were not there time would not be of much use. If the rate of atoms were to become contingent and sort of jump around, then you might as well give up the notion of time. If there were nothing which would follow that order, there wouldn't be any use to think of it.

Q: You said that time is an abstraction, which arises out of representation or out of thought. But also it seems that thought presupposes time; thought seems to be a process in time. In a way it's circular.

Bohm: They go in a circle, yes. If we admit that thought is a material process, and if we think of matter as moving in an order in time, then that would suggest that thought will also be moving in that time.

Q: In our discussion of thought, aren't we assuming time to some extent?

Bohm: As we now have it, every thought assumes time. Whether we discuss thought or anything else, we always take time for granted. And we take for granted the notion that everything exists in time. We don't take for granted that time is an abstraction and a representation, but we take for granted that time is of the essence – reality – and that everything is existing in time, including thought. There's some correctness to that, in the sense that its order of succession can be put in terms of time.

Q: Time is an essential part of Newtonian physics, but what about modern physics?

Bohm: It's still playing a basic part, but it's not so clear what it means. When you get to relativity it becomes dependent on the speed of the measuring instrument. And in quantum mechanics it becomes indeterminate to some extent. But the basic concept of time has not yet been altered – it is still taken as the basic frame on which everything is put.

Q: In psychological thought, what is the error concerning time?

Bohm: What I said was, that in order for notions of time to be really coherently relevant and applicable, we need to have some suitable orders of succession to which they will fit. If there were no orders of succession, which were all synchronous and corresponding, then the notion of time would be quite useless.

It's not so obvious, even in physics – it took a long while in physics just to get clocks that you could count on. But psychologically the thing is far more complex. As you know, in your psychological experience one moment can seem a year, a long time can seem a short time, and so on; it's not quite so simple as with physics. The whole process or movement is infinitely complex and very subtle. Everything is changing every moment, and the possibility of keeping track of it is nil.

You can imagine that between this moment now and the next moment there is a stretch; then it is really space by which you are representing time. When you say 'ahead of me is the future', that a spatial analogy. You imagine the future stretches ahead and the past is behind. But the past is nowhere. The future is nowhere. Still, your experience is that 'back there' is the past and 'ahead of me' is the future. That's a way of representing time, but it also seems to be a way of experiencing it.

So we seem to be moving from the past toward the future. I've said, though, that that *experience* isn't making sense because the future doesn't exist. It isn't spread out before you. And the past is not there behind you. All you have is the present. When it comes to the psychological fact, the only fact you have is the present, the *now*.

Q: What about the physical fact?

Bohm: Even the physical fact must start from the present. Physics can establish a fact of the order of succession. But that order cannot be so nicely established psychologically. You can hardly remember very much of what happened in the past, and it has been proved that it's mostly invented anyway. And the future is an expectation which is seldom realized. You can count on a physical fact, such as we can meet at an agreed upon time if our watches are working right. But you can't count on any such thing with psychological time. Therefore, we begin to see that it isn't so coherent.

Relativity theory would say that the whole of time is one big block, like space. But then you can't quite understand why you experience this moment now. One view is to say that you are like a train going through time, but then you've introduced another kind of time. You've slipped it in again. So the best way to look at physics is to say that it has made an abstract representation which allows you to keep track of the order of succession. The order of succession is really the fact.

The next question we have to raise is: when there is an order of succession, is that order necessary or contingent? In physics we are looking for what are called 'laws of nature'. We try to find necessary orders of succession, such as the law of motion. We call these laws. The word 'law', however, is an unfortunate word because it suggests a legislator, and all that. But it could be called 'a natural regularity' in the order of succession. In physics we discover such regularity in the necessary order of succession. If there were no necessity in this order, the notion of time might as well be given up anyway.

When you say 'I expect to arrive at success in changing myself in the future', you are counting on some order of necessity in that succession – a series of steps in which you will necessarily arrive at a better state. Actually it is all contingent; that is the fact. I may intend to arrive there, but I may arrive somewhere else altogether.

So what point does that order of time have? It's entirely imagined. You may say 'I'm going to take a trip and go through a series of cities between here and San Francisco, and it will take a certain amount of time to go through them. I'm going to go through this one first and then this one and then this one.' And if you have a good map, that is what will actually happen. On the other hand, if you say 'I'm going to go through a series of steps in self-improvement', it won't happen.

Q: It's deception, isn't it?

Bohm: Yes, it's a kind of deception.

Q: It's sort of like trying to climb the rainbow.

Bohm: In fact, all these psychological steps are rainbows that

233

you're chasing. Therefore, we say that it doesn't look as if this notion of time has nearly as much meaning psychologically as physically. It has a little bit of meaning psychologically because it takes time to speak, time to think; the physiological process of thought takes time; we have all sorts of body clocks, and thought is tied to that, and so on. So it works up to a point. It's not entirely meaningless, but there's not much meaning. You can't say that it's of the essence.

Q: Earlier we said that the mental and the physical are not really that different. But now we're making a distinction of time in the physical area and time in the psychological areas.

Bohm: Even in the physical we could say that wherever we get to something so infinitely complex that we can't find an order of necessity, it becomes dubious. The people who work in quantum mechanics are facing that. They are saying that depending on your measurement it becomes somewhat uncertain what the time is. So there is already in physics a limit to the order of necessity, although it still works up to a point. But in the psychological domain, the attempt to use this order is causing a great deal of confusion.

Q: We're suggesting that part of the psychological domain is an illusion, and that's why time doesn't work there, why time is really not of the essence. Time with self is of no use, because the self is a rainbow. But is there another psychological domain which would be more real, where time still would not work?

Bohm: There may be. We could say that if we start to analyse the material process of the body, as scientists are doing, time will certainly carry us a long way. When we come to the mind, however, we see the problem I mentioned: this big puzzle that the past seems to be behind us and the future ahead. But that's just the rainbow. Then we say 'OK, it doesn't seem to be coherent to apply time to this rainbow chasing'. So where are the past and the future psychologically? Even physically we can't really get hold of them; although working with those concepts we can make some sense of the succession.

What suggests itself is that psychologically – and perhaps eventually for the deepest level physically – we can't use time as the essence. Rather, the moment *now* is the essence, because all the past and the future that we ever will know are in this moment. The past and the future are now – namely, in so far as it has left any impression., whatever has happened is now. And our expectations are now. Thus we could say that now may be the starting point.

One picture you could make of an electron would be that it sort of flashes into and out of existence so fast that when picked up in the usual equipment it looks continuously existent. It might have a certain regularity, so that it appears to obey an order of necessity. But it might be that it is basically creative; the creative act may create this order of necessity.

Q: Would that mean that any time we escape from the now we are trying to change what is necessary?

Bohm: We are trying to push the order of necessity into the time order. We're trying to make a change in this order. But we are in an area where that sort of abstraction, or that sort of representation, cannot work. Even in physics we have to admit that this was always a representation, that the actual experience was always now.

Q: Then any escaping from the now would be disorder, incoherence and violence?

Bohm: What this escape amounts to is that all these reflexes – which are the 'past' – have affected our perception very strongly so that we *see* differently. We don't see the now as anything more than a flash in this time.

Q: Is there a difference between necessity in the order of succession and necessity in the moment?

Bohm: I would suggest that necessity in the moment is a kind of creative necessity, as we talked about in relation to art, where within the contingency there is a creative act. But in matter the creation is *re*creation again and again – similar but different; similar enough so that the form holds. In the psychic domain, though, this similarity doesn't hold except in thought, because thought is based on memory, and memory is just that thing which tries to hold this similarity. Memory has a base in the material process, and the material process is able to carry the similarity. It makes a record. Is it clear what I mean?

Q: The past, the present, and the future are one motion. If you look at a slow motion film of somebody taking a step, you see a movement of past, present and future, but it's one movement.

Bohm: It is one movement. We talked about emptiness containing energy. And it may be that the movement is basically creative, in the sense that we talked about insight or creativity being from this total source. It may be that there is a source beyond this level of matter from which creativity emerges, producing similarity and difference. And in a certain mode of perception, picking up a certain part of this process will create a sense of continuity.

We've said before that the past and the future are images contained in thought. Thought ties those images together with the present to give a sense of movement and *continuity*. Using the example of a film – a cine-camera records a series of somewhat different images. When played back they give a sense of motion. This happens because the brain does not distinguish images that are more than, say, a tenth or so of a second apart; so when a lot of these images are seen rapidly they are sensed as continuity. Similarly, a lot of grains of flowing sand might look like water, continuous.

You can see that this sense of continuity arises from thought, which puts it all together.

Q: You're saying that in the psychological domain the continuity is non-existent and only created by thought. Continuity is inferred from the material realm, where continuity does seem to exist because of the arising of similarities.

Bohm: That's right. In the psychological domain, whatever continuity exists is held by thought – and not very coherently.

Q: Then the difference between the psychological and the physical domains is that the psychological has this infinite complexity?

Bohm: It's very subtle and complex. But maybe the depth of the physical domain is equally subtle and complex. That's the suggestion. We're drawing inferences and making suggestions to consider.

Now, this ties with thought. We discussed the observer and the observed being perceived as separate, with a space between them. But we said that that is in the image. If it were not an image, that separation would imply that there would be time to act, that it would take time to cross the space. And, having that space in time, the observer would be independent enough so that he could think about the observed a little while and then do something.

But if that separation is just simply an image, when in fact the observer and the observed are all one thought process, then whatever you call 'the observer' has already been affected by the thing he wants to observe. Namely, if he wants to observe anger he has already been affected by anger in a distorted way. So he doesn't have any time. There is no space. There is no time. There is nothing but thought, which has been affected by anger. And this requires an insight, which would free the whole process.

Wherever there is a certain space and a certain independence, it leaves the possibility of taking time. In the physical sense that coheres, it can work coherently – the further away something is the more time you have to deal with it, the more time you have to think. But in the thought process the thing is so entangled – involved and folded together – that there isn't that time, there isn't that space.

Q: It's as you said about Leibniz having the idea that space is the co-existence. In a way, in the moment things co-exist. And if you have an insight in the moment, would you then have a new kind of co-existence where everything would move together?

Bohm: Yes. it would co-exist in a coherent way, creatively; that is the suggestion.

Now, all of this might also have to arise in the collective context of a dialogue. We probably wouldn't get into it right away; but if we were able to pursue this, sustain this dialogue properly, then people might get into that too – experiencing time differently together, and so on.

I think all of that is possible, is open. But what we need to do about time is to begin the same way as we deal with anger. We have to begin to see how our experience of time is affected by thought. To begin to get into it we find those thoughts which are affecting our way of sensing time and put them into words and observe carefully. We have to see that time, which seems to be there of its own accord without thought, would not be there without thought – not psychological time. No time would be there, really, without thought.

The point is to get an insight into this. I think that the liberation from this process, from this incoherent kind of thought, requires bringing in all these questions – all that we've been talking about, including time. As long as we accept time and take it for granted, we will be constantly slipping back.

Q: Is time more primary than the self-image?

Bohm: It probably is. Time is a process based on our whole notion of being able to order the world, which includes the self. With anything you intend to do, you begin to project time – you begin to bring this thing in. There's a place where it may make sense. But seeing that it generally does not, getting that clear, is crucial to the whole thing.

Q: So time is a misrepresentation of successions?

Bohm: It may be in a certain area a correct representation. But when it is extended too far it becomes a misrepresentation.

Q: Yesterday you put the question of what could reach the substance, the structure. What can actually get to the chemistry of it all?

Bohm: That would again be perception or insight. And insight, we've already seen, is beyond time. We've seen that insight cannot take time.

Q: Would it be correct to say that dialogue is the doorway to insight?

Bohm: For insight together we need dialogue. Individually a person can have insight; but we need it together, because now the civilization has reached a stage where it cannot

239

proceed in the other way. In general we needed it anyhow, but we now really need it.

Q: You said earlier that the self-image, the 'I Am', has a sense of godlikeness. And time also brings in the notion of godlikeness, because if there is time then you have control – a way to order things. I wonder what's behind this strong impulse to want to be godlike?

Bohm: You can imagine that this image could somehow arise in the child. And once the image arises it becomes a reflex. It would be very hard to trace the source of all this, but all of these elements come together and they form links which support each other. Then it's so exhilarating that the body itself wants to hold it.

Q: Also, once you have an 'I', or the sense of oneself as separate, you're almost going to have to be godlike to get by.

Bohm: That may be true, too. But it ties together – if it were not for this notion of psychological time there would be no meaning to the self-image, because there would be no time in which the self-image could do anything.

Q: Essentially what we've been talking about is that the problem of man is thought, this self-image which is so faulty. The 'self' is the complexity and depth of all this. Thought is partaking of itself as the self.

Bohm: That's right, thought is constantly trying to grasp things and to bring order to them. And it would try to grasp itself, because it sees the inferential evidence of itself. And so it explains itself as coming from a source – a source which is an image, which has time to act, which has psychological time, and so on. If all of that were not there, then these incoherent things in the process of thought wouldn't occur.

But that requires insight into this whole thing we've been discussing. And that insight would open the door to freedom, collectively as well as individually – to friendship and fellowship and love.

I think that we should close now. We've covered a lot of ground, and I hope that we will be able to proceed with this throughout the year and meet again.

INDEX

INDEX

violence 17, 25, 61, 64, 226
'vision of dialogue' 203, 205–7,
  209

wars 2, 3, 4, 6
'watching' our thoughts 142–3
wealth (and money) 165
weapons 2
well-being 46, 118
'what seems to be'/'what is'
  15–16
whole 94, 115, 118–19, 123;
  incoherence and 56–8
withdrawal process (drugs)
  153–4

words: bringing out memory
  88–9; communicated (in
  thought process) 90–1;
  expressed thoughts 81–6,
  149–50; and images 154–5;
  insight and 149; use of
  language 87, 88–9; yelled
  message 81–3
world-self (separation) 210
world in chaos 1–3, 14

yelling (responses to) 74–83
  passim

Zionism (assumptions) 190, 203